# NORTHWEST TERRITORIES

Volume 12, Number 1 / 1985
ALASKA GEOGRAPHIC®

## The Alaska Geographic Society

*To teach many more to better know and use our natural resources*

**Editor:** Penny Rennick
**Associate Editor:** Kathy Doogan
**Designer:** Sandra Harner
**Cartographer:** Jon Hersh

ALASKA GEOGRAPHIC®, ISSN 0361-1353, is published quarterly by The Alaska Geographic Society, Anchorage, Alaska 99509-6057. Second-class postage paid in Edmonds, Washington 98020-3588. Printed in U.S.A. Copyright© 1985 by The Alaska Geographic Society. All rights reserved. Registered trademark: Alaska Geographic. ISSN 0361-1353; Key title Alaska Geographic.

THE ALASKA GEOGRAPHIC SOCIETY is a nonprofit organization exploring new frontiers of knowledge across the lands of the polar rim, learning how other men and other countries live in their Norths, putting the geography book back in the classroom, exploring new methods of teaching and learning — sharing in the excitement of discovery in man's wonderful new world north of 51° 16 '.

MEMBERS OF THE SOCIETY RECEIVE *ALASKA GEOGRAPHIC®*, a quality magazine which devotes each quarterly issue to monographic in-depth coverage of a northern geographic region or resource-oriented subject.

MEMBERSHIP DUES in The Alaska Geographic Society are $30 per year; $34 to non-U.S. addresses. (Eighty percent of each year's dues is for a one-year subscription to *ALASKA GEOGRAPHIC®.)* Order from The Alaska Geographic Society, Box 4-EEE, Anchorage, Alaska 99509-6057; (907) 274-0521.

MATERIAL SOUGHT: The editors of *ALASKA GEOGRAPHIC®* seek a wide variety of informative material on the lands north of 51° 16 ' on geographic subjects — anything to do with resources and their uses (with heavy emphasis on quality color photography) — from Alaska, northern Canada, Siberia, Japan — all geographic areas that have a relationship to Alaska in a physical or economic sense. We do not want material done in excessive scientific terminology. A query to the editors is suggested. Payments are made for all material upon publicaton.

CHANGE OF ADDRESS: The post office does not automatically forward *ALASKA GEOGRAPHIC®* when you move. To ensure continuous service, notify us six weeks before moving. Send us your new address and zip code (and moving date), your old address and zip code, and if possible send a mailing label from a copy of *ALASKA GEOGRAPHIC®*. Send this information to *ALASKA GEOGRAPHIC®* Mailing Offices, 130 Second Avenue South, Edmonds, Washington 98020-3588.

MAILING LISTS: We have begun making our members' names and addresses available to carefully screened publications and companies whose products and activities might be of interest of you. If you would prefer not to receive such mailings, please so advise us, and include your mailing label (or your name and address if label is not available).

**STATEMENT OF OWNERSHIP MANAGEMENT and CIRCULATION**

*ALASKA GEOGRAPHIC®* is a quarterly publication, home offices Box 4-EEE, Anchorage, Alaska 99509. Editor is Penny Rennick. Publisher is The Alaska Geographic Society, a nonprofit Alaska organization, Box 4-EEE, Anchorage, Alaska 99509. Owners are Robert A. Henning and Phyllis G. Henning, Box 4-EEE, Anchorage, Alaska 99509. Robert A. Henning and Phyllis G. Henning, husband and wife, are owners of 100 percent of all common stock outstanding. *ALASKA GEOGRAPHIC®* has a membership of 16,312.
I certify that statements above are correct and complete.
ROBERT A. HENNING
Chief Editor

The Library of Congress has cataloged this serial publication as follows:

Alaska Geographic. v.1-
[Anchorage, Alaska Geographic Society] 1972-
v. ill. (part col.). 23 x 31 cm.
Quarterly.
Official publication of the Alaska Geographic Society.
Key title: Alaska geographic, ISSN 0361-1353.

1. Alaska—Description and travel—1959- —Periodicals.    I. Alaska Geographic Society.

F901.A266        917.98 '04 '505        72-92087
                                         MARC-S

Library of Congress        75[7912]

**Cover** — *A family returns from a midnight fishing trip at Arctic Bay, population 387, on the west shore of Borden Peninusla on northern Baffin Island. Although the area has been occupied since prehistoric times, construction of a Hudson's Bay Co. post here in the 1920s gave impetus to development of a modern settlement.* (Lyn Hancock)

**Previous page** — *Ice and water create a lacy collar for Nelson Head at the southern tip of Banks Island, westernmost of the Arctic Islands.* (Lyn Hancock)

**Editor's note:**

Geographic statistics used in this issue, such as land and freshwater area and length of rivers, are the most accurate and up-to-date available at press time. However, detailed mapping of Northwest Territories is still being done. As the scale of mapping is refined, and more accurate locational control points for mapping are established, these figures will change.

Most populations are based on figures from June 1980. Exceptions are Aklavik, Arctic Red River, Fort McPherson, Inuvik, Paulatuk, Tuktoyaktuk, and Sachs Harbour; figures for these communities were taken from the 1984 edition of *The MILEPOST®*.

**About This Issue:**

Canada's immense Northwest Territories comprises some of the most beautiful and remote land in North America. To compile this issue, we called upon Richard Harrington, frequent contributor to the *ALASKA GEOGRAPHIC®*, for his appreciation and understanding of the people and their land. He spent many months selecting authors to share their knowledge and photographers to share their impressions of this diverse country and the people who inhabit it.

We thank those authors: Dr. J. Lewis Robinson, who provides an overview of the geography of the region, from forests to ice caps; Dr. Joseph MacInnis, for his account of what it is like to visit the ocean floor, beneath the ice of Arctic Canada; Fred Bruemmer, who describes the region's animals and how they adapt to their northern environment; Dr. Robert McGhee, who provides information on the prehistoric peoples of Northwest Territories, and George Swinton for his discussion of the art of the Inuit, then and now; Dr. R. Michael Easton and Gerry Wingenbach, for their contributions on geology and mineral resources of the Canadian Arctic; Lyn Harrington, who gives us a detailed account of hundreds of years of exploration and the relentless search for the Northwest Passage; Capt. Thomas Pullen, for sharing his experiences with modern icebreakers in the Northwest Passage; and John Goddard, who provides a look at the people of Northwest Territories, how they live and how they would like to live.

We also thank the many photographers whose images capture the beauty, isolation, and spirit of this land and its people; and we are grateful to our reviewers, Ann Taylor and Dr. Robert Janes of the Government of the Northwest Territories, for their comments.

# TABLE OF CONTENTS

*Inuit gather at a summer camp on the west coast of the Boothia Peninsula, northernmost point on mainland North America. In the past, Inuit moved from camp to camp, seeking the natural bounty that sustained their subsistence lifestyle. Today many of the people are moving to established communities where they strive to adapt to new ways. (Richard Harrington)*

# INTRODUCTION

*Editor's note: Richard Harrington is a noted Canadian free-lance writer and photographer. Although he has traveled to almost every country in the world, he is constantly drawn back to the Canadian Arctic, and he has written four books about the land and people of the region.*

*By Richard Harrington*

The five administrative regions presently comprising Canada's Northwest Territories — Inuvik, Fort Smith, Kitikmeot, Baffin and Keewatin — are but remnants of a much larger piece of real estate, from which several provinces and Yukon Territory were shaped. There's still plenty left, for the Northwest Territories occupies the whole upper third of the country, stretching through four time zones, from Greenland nearly to Alaska, and from the 60th parallel of latitude to the North Pole.

Such a vast area — more than twice the size of Alaska — is bound to hold contrasts in terrain. Bleak, treeless snowcaps of Ellesmere Island are the highest mountains east of the Rockies; nearby blue waters are lively with bits of the polar ice pack; arctic prairies in summer glow with brilliant short-lived blooms and in winter are ice deserts of whirling ground storms and whiteouts.

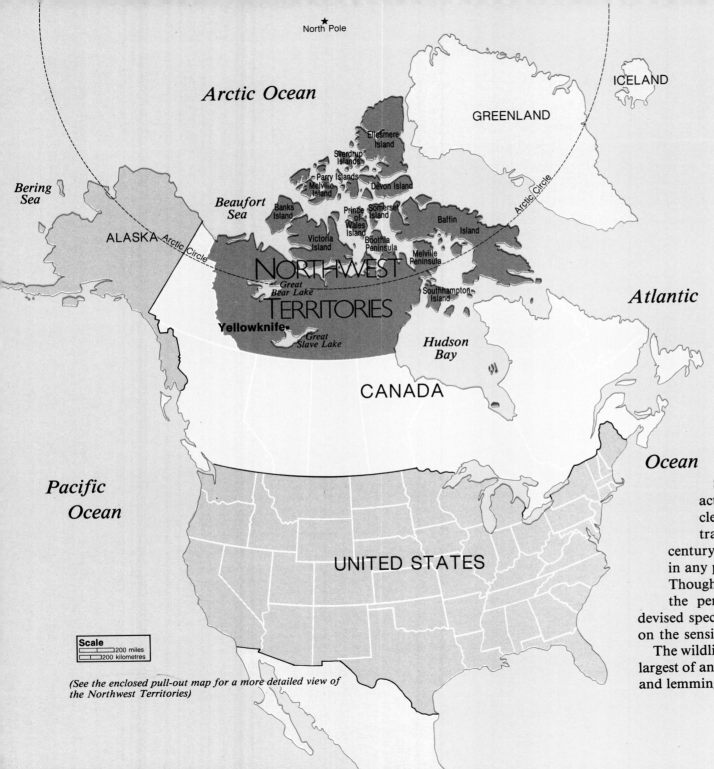

North Pole

*Arctic Ocean*

ICELAND

GREENLAND

Ellesmere
Island

Sverdrup
Islands

Parry Islands

Melville
Island

Devon Island

*Bering
Sea*

*Beaufort
Sea*

Banks
Island

Prince
of
Wales
Island

Somerset
Island

Baffin
Island

ALASKA Arctic Circle

Victoria
Island

Boothia
Peninsula

Melville
Peninsula

Arctic Circle

NORTHWEST

*Great
Bear Lake*

Southhampton
Island

*Atlantic*

TERRITORIES

**Yellowknife**

*Great
Slave Lake*

*Hudson
Bay*

*Ocean*

CANADA

*Pacific
Ocean*

UNITED STATES

**Scale**
200 miles
200 kilometres

*(See the enclosed pull-out map for a more detailed view of
the Northwest Territories)*

The tree line wavers, broad-leaved poplars giving way to the taiga of pointed spruce, peltlike over the hills and filling some river valleys. Spruce dwindle to little sticks, and these to dwarf birch and willow, centuries old but only a foot high. Trees yield to grasses and mosses and sedges beside the innumerable ponds that overlie the permafrost and rock.

Such endurance seems hardy but is actually fragile in the extreme. A vehicle traveling over the tundra leaves tracks that persist for more than a century. The ecology is now a major factor in any plans for the Northwest Territories. Though gas and oil are known to lie beneath the permafrost, drilling companies have devised special equipment to reduce the impact on the sensitive environment.

The wildlife of the Territories ranges from the largest of animals, whales, to the smallest, shrews and lemmings. On land, moose, Barren Ground grizzlies and polar bears are largest, though once woolly mammoths and giant beavers laid their bones in bogs.

Far more abundant than any of these, or the mice that live in the grass roots or the ground squirrels that pop out of their burrows or the great herds of caribou that ford northern streams on ancient migration routes, are the millions of birds that scream and wheel around bird precipices, fighting for space on narrow ledges, or haunt nesting sites beside ponds and sloughs. Outnumbering them all are the myriad mosquitoes which continue to defend their territory against explorers of every kind, settlers and visitors.

From Asia came people over Bering Strait, by the shrinking land bridge or in skin boats. They spread south into warmer climes, becoming Indians. When later contingents arrived, they were obliged to accept the northern rim of the continent. The Canadian Eskimos now call themselves Inuit (singular, Inuk) and the northern Indians are the Dene. Both words mean "people."

From Europe came first the explorers, chiefly British, and then the fur traders. From the south came the entrepreneurs, the police, the geologists, the social workers and the administrators. And the scientists. A joke went around that an Inuit family comprised two parents, two children and a researcher.

Some of them stayed to add to the amalgam and to increase the sparse population. The explorers came in their unheated, unhealthful

*Conifers, brush, and countless ponds cover the lowlands of the Mackenzie Delta in northwestern Northwest Territories. (Lyn Hancock)*

Mount Sir James MacBrien,
highest point in mainland
Northwest Territories at
9,062 feet (2,762 meters),
crowns the Selwyn and
Mackenzie mountains that
straddle the divide between
the region and Yukon
Territory to the west.
Extensive melting from
glaciers behind the
mountain feed milky green
Glacier Lake in the
foreground. (George Luste)

wooden ships, and many died on the bleak shores. Others paddled their bark canoes or trudged thousands of weary miles across the Barren Lands, creating their own maps as they went. Each filled in some dotted lines, with certainty outlining the channels, peninsulas and islands that form the gigantic jigsaw puzzle of the High Arctic.

A barren land, thought the explorers. No good for agriculture, thought the farm minds of the south. Better leave it to Indian and Eskimo trappers. Or to prospectors.

The quest for the Arctic's mineral wealth began with Martin Frobisher, who loaded his vessels with worthless pyrites, fool's gold.

Modern prospectors search with Geiger counters and magnetometers, and set off seismic explosions, on land or at sea, drilling from ice platforms, from ships or from man-made islands. The sight would make the old sea dogs of the British Admiralty rub their eyes in amazement.

The Northwest Territories has developed considerably in the last half-century but is far from being a finished product. Where the frost-bitten explorers toiled and suffered, aircraft now speed into every corner of the vast domain. At high cost, admittedly.

Aircraft have largely displaced ship traffic, except for scows on the long Mackenzie River and annual supply boats along the coast. Gravel roads poke north year by year. There is even one railway reaching the south shore of Great Slave Lake. Should the known mineral resources of the Territories be needed badly enough to justify the huge cost of extracting and shipping, more ways will be found to get them to market. In the meantime, what's the hurry? The minerals will store nicely in their rockbound treasure chest, hiding their glitter until their day dawns.

Changes can't come fast enough for some, those who have felt they were living in a colony, frustrated by government in faraway Ottawa. Inuit and Dene and immigrants from the south are acquiring more autonomy. They share the same social benefits as their countrymen Outside, and sometimes more. Permanent residents have come to terms with isolation and a cool climate, and spend a lifetime extolling the virtues of "a solitude that fills the soul."

*Pastels brighten the houses along this street in Yellowknife, population about 10,000, on North Arm of Great Slave Lake. The town became the capital of the Northwest Territories in 1967.*
*(Richard Harrington)*

*The cheerful grin of a young Inuk from Paulatuk, population 95, welcomes shoppers to the make-believe store at her school. The tiny community, at the south end of Darnley Bay on the arctic coast of the mainland, takes its name from the native term for "soot of coal." Earlier inhabitants of the area burned coal for heat.*
*(Lyn Hancock)*

*The Dempster Highway
stretches northeastward
462 miles (743 kilometers)
from Dawson City in
Yukon Territory to Inuvik
in the Mackenzie Delta in
Northwest Territories.*
*(Charles Kay)*

*Conifers, birches and willows characterize the boreal forests, or taiga, of the Northwest Territories. The boundary between the boreal forest and the tundra of the Arctic twists and turns across the Northwest Territories from the Mackenzie Delta to a point on Hudson Bay just south of the Northwest Territories-Manitoba border. (Fred Bruemmer)*

# THE LAY OF THE LAND

*Editor's note: Dr. J. Lewis Robinson's familiarity with the North dates back to 1943, when he was the first professional geographer to be employed by the federal Northwest Territories Administration. He is currently professor of geography at the University of British Columbia in Vancouver.*

*By Dr. J. Lewis Robinson*

The Northwest Territories covers 1,322,834 square miles (3,426,320 square kilometers) of the Canadian mainland and Arctic Islands — more than twice the area of Alaska. This large and diverse region stretches nearly 1,700 miles (2,730 kilometers) north to south, from 60 degrees north to Cape Columbia on northern Ellesmere Island, and about 2,000 miles (3,220 kilometers) east to west, from eastern Baffin Island to the border of Yukon Territory. The land area does not include thousands of square miles of water in the many channels and straits among the Arctic Islands, nor the area of Hudson Bay. Some Canadian maps claim a pie-shaped wedge of ice floes in the Arctic Ocean stretching to the geographical North Pole, but others claim only any islands that may be discovered in this sector.

Northwest Territories is a geographical misnomer, as today much of the region is actually

*A group of river runners ride their rubber rafts through rapids on the Slave River, which connects waters of Lake Athabasca in northern Alberta and Saskatchewan to Great Slave Lake in the Northwest Territories. (Richard Harrington)*

*A patch of red snow nestles at the base of a rocky outcrop in the Northwest Territories. The snow's rusty appearance is due to the presence of red-pigmented algae which are capable of producing their own food through photosynthesis. Long, sunny days of summer encourage the algae's rapid reproduction, creating large areas of red snow. (Fred Bruemmer)*

in northeastern Canada. In the 19th century the Northwest Territories included the area of the present prairie provinces and all of northern Canada. Yukon Territory, in the real northwest, became a separate political unit in 1898, and Saskatchewan and Alberta became provinces in 1905, leaving the remainder of the Northwest Territories mainly in northcentral and northeastern Canada. The original name was never changed to describe its present location.

The Northwest Territories' Arctic Islands are more northerly than Alaska. Cape Columbia, at the northern tip of Ellesmere Island on the Arctic Ocean, lies at 83 degrees north latitude. Even the northernmost part of the mainland, Boothia Peninsula, is at 72 degrees north, one degree farther north than Point Barrow, Alaska.

It is not surprising that such a large area contains a complete range of physical environments, from the highest mountains in eastern North America to broad, flat plains. The mountain system that extends through the eastern Arctic Islands has snow- and ice-covered uplands and peaks 5,000 to more than 9,000 feet (1,500 to 2,750 meters) in height. Northwest Territories' highest point is in the United States Range on northern Ellesmere Island, where Barbeau Peak rises 8,911 feet (2,716 meters), and some maps show unnamed peaks exceeding 9,500 feet (2,900 meters). Mount Sir James MacBrien (9,062 feet; 2,762 meters) is the high point of the rugged Selwyn and Mackenzie mountain ranges to the west, along the border of Yukon Territory.

Three of the world's largest islands are located in the Arctic Archipelago. Baffin Island, which covers nearly 196,000 square miles (507,454 square

*An early-morning frost in August covers a sand
beach in the Barren Lands. (R. Michael Easton)*

*Blossoms of the spider plant, a member of the saxifrage family, brighten the tundra of the Northwest Territories. Most plants of the Arctic are perennials that store nutrients from season to season.*
*(Fred Bruemmer)*

kilometers) ranks fifth, while 82,114-square-mile (212,687-square-kilometer) Ellesmere Island — northernmost point in the Territories — and 81,925-square-mile (212,198-square-kilometer) Victoria Island, rank ninth and tenth.

Small permanent icecaps, remnants of the last Ice Age, cover much of the eastern Arctic Islands. From these shrinking icecaps, broad glaciers discharge to scenic, fjord-lined coasts. In contrast, the central Arctic Islands and northern mainland are made up of flat, poorly drained, lake-dotted plains hundreds of miles in extent, broken only by hills of a few hundred feet or steep-sided low plateaus of about 1,000 feet (300 meters) in height.

The western region of the Northwest Territories, which consists primarily of the broad valley of the Mackenzie River, is a dramatic geographic contrast to the Far North. The two largest lakes in the Territories are located in this region. Great Bear Lake, the largest, covers 12,120 square miles (31,400 square kilometers) and is the ninth largest lake in the world. Great Slave Lake, Northwest Territories' second largest, encompasses 10,979 square miles (28,438 square kilometers), plunges to a depth of 2,000 feet (610 meters), and is considered the source of the region's longest river, the Mackenzie.

The Mackenzie River, 1,081 miles (1,740 kilometers) long from Great Slave Lake to the Beaufort Sea and one to three miles wide, flows between steep gravel banks through a wide forested valley, filled with glacially deposited sand and gravel. The Mackenzie Valley narrows from about 250 miles (400 kilometers) wide northwest of Great Slave Lake to about 40 miles (65 kilometers) wide between the Franklin and Mackenzie

mountains west of Great Bear Lake. Major rivers in the Mackenzie system include the 258-mile (415-kilometer) Slave River, which empties into Great Slave Lake, and the Liard River.

The Coppermine River rises in the central plains and flows through a steep-sided valley to Coronation Gulf, 525 miles (845 kilometers) to the northwest on the Arctic Ocean. Other important rivers in the Northwest Territories include the 605-mile (974-kilometer) Back River, which flows through the lake-dotted plains; the Anderson River, whose winding 430-mile (692-kilometer) path makes its way to Wood Bay on the Beaufort Sea; and the 350-mile (563-kilometer) South Nahanni River, which flows through the center of Nahanni National Park.

Permafrost covers the arctic regions of the Northwest Territories. This permanently frozen subsurface is a remnant of the Glacial Age, when a large icecap covered the entire area and caused the soil, gravel and rock beneath to become frozen to a depth of several hundred feet. At present, only a few inches or feet on the surface melt in summer. Within the permafrost area, a variety of unique land forms exist, such as pingoes, conical, ice-cored hills; ice wedges, which will possibly affect pipeline routes; and patterned ground where frost-fractured rock creates polygonal shapes.

Dramatic variations exist between the climates of the northeastern and northwestern sections of the Northwest Territories. The northeast — north of a diagonal line extending approximately from

*A harsh climate creates bleak moonscapes in the limestone plains and valleys of Somerset Island, north of Boothia Peninsula. (Fred Bruemmer)*

*Hikers gaze over the South Nahanni River Valley in southwestern Northwest Territories. The river, named for the Nahanni Indian word meaning "people over there far away," drops 3,000 feet (915 meters) in 300 miles (480 kilometers) from the border with Yukon Territory to its junction with the Liard River. The upper river valley, shown here, is not included in Nahanni National Park.*
(George Luste)

*Cotton grass, also known as arctic cotton, grows in profusion among the muskeg and black spruce of southern Northwest Territories. (Fred Bruemmer)*

*Large areas of southwestern Northwest Territories are covered with muskeg and black spruce.*
*(Richard Harrington)*

*Travelers push their canoes over the quickly melting ice of Mackay Lake, one of myriad lakes and ponds in the vast expanse of the Barren Lands. The lake, north of Great Slave Lake, was first seen by a white man in 1771 when Samuel Hearne, on foot, traversed northern Canada from Churchill on Hudson Bay to the mouth of the Coppermine River on the Arctic Coast.*
(George Luste)

Churchill, Manitoba, to the mouth of the Mackenzie River — has a genuine arctic climate in which there is no summer. The northwestern part — mainly the Mackenzie River Valley — has a subarctic climate with a short summer, much like Alaska's Interior.

In the past, the Arctic as a climatic region was defined simply as anywhere north of the Arctic Circle (67 degrees north). This definition is now known to be misleading. Because the Mackenzie Valley and interior Alaska are on the same latitude as the Keewatin District — northwest of Hudson Bay — and southern Baffin Island, they receive the same number of hours of midsummer daylight; however, the regions to the west enjoy much warmer summer temperatures. Climatologists today define the Arctic as an area where average monthly (not daily) temperatures are less than 50 degrees (10 degrees C) in July. By this definition, all of northeastern Northwest Territories has an arctic climate.

The principal difference between an arctic and subarctic climate is summer temperature. From June to August the Mackenzie Valley may be crossed by occasional relatively mild air masses from the North Pacific or the northern plains of the continent's interior. These air masses can raise daily summer temperatures into the 70s, and sometimes 80s (20 degrees to 32 degrees C). In contrast, the northeast is surrounded by ice-covered seas and channels in June and by cold water in July and August. The northeast is far from any source of warm air; therefore daily midsummer temperatures are usually in the 40s and 50s (5 degrees to 15 degrees C), and only occasionally reach into the 60s (15 degrees to 21 degrees C).

An interesting climatic anomaly occurs on northern Ellesmere Island, in the area of Hazen Plateau. The region is known as a thermal oasis where maximum summer temperatures, normally less than 50 degrees (10 degrees C) on this arctic island, have been known to reach 65 degrees (18

*A hiker follows a trail in Auyuittuq National Park on Baffin Island's Cumberland Peninsula. Established in 1972, the park was originally named Baffin Island National Park, but in 1975 Parks Canada chose the new name, an Inuit word meaning "the place which does not melt."*
(Lyn Hancock)

NORTH POLE — 1841

OAK LAKE — 1497

OTTAWA — 1219

NEW YORK —

MOOSE JAW — 1598

TRANSCONA — 1345

PARRY SOUND

*More than 1,800 miles (2,900 kilometers) south of the North Pole, the village of Lake Harbour, population about 300, nestles among the hills of Meta Incognita Peninsula on southern Baffin Island. (Fred Bruemmer)*

degrees C). The exceptionally warm temperatures are attributed to the surrounding south-facing slopes, which absorb the warmth of the sun. Additional heat is reflected off Lake Hazen, which lies at approximately 82 degrees north and is noted as the largest body of fresh water north of 76 degrees.

The Northwest Territories is not a land of deep and continuous snow. The central and northern Arctic Islands record the least amount of average annual precipitation in Canada, less than five inches. Most of Northwest Territories is covered all winter with granular snow which blows from place to place, making it difficult to record whether new snow is falling or old snow is blowing. In former days, Natives sometimes had to search to find snow of sufficient depth and consistency to cut blocks for snow houses. In summer, when temperatures are warmer, the small amount of precipitation falls as drizzle.

Climatic differences in summer result in distinct vegetation between the arctic northeast and subarctic northwest. Trees do not grow in the Arctic; plant life consists mainly of tussocks, lichen and other low-growing tundra vegetation. The northwestern region, located south of the northern tree line, is the site of the Northwest Territories' 211,000 square miles (550,000 square kilometers) of spruce, birch, aspen and alder forest.

The physical environment boundaries are also cultural boundaries, separating the homelands of Indians and Eskimos. Canadian Eskimos (Inuit) inhabit the treeless arctic region, which covers about one million square miles, while the Indians (Dene) live in the forested, subarctic Mackenzie River Valley.

*Weathering has produced a magnificent display of nature's handiwork on these cliffs near Baillarge Bay on northern Baffin Island.* (Richard Harrington)

# A View From Under the Ice

## By Dr. Joseph B. MacInnis

*Editor's note: Dr. Joseph B. MacInnis is the first man to dive and film beneath the North Pole. For more than 20 years he has been studying the relationship between man and the sea, focusing recently on such issues as pollution, energy and resources. Because of his concern for increased public awareness of the oceans, he has written many books and articles on the subject, and has been host and scientific consultant for a number of television programs concerning the sea.*

Pushed by forces of wind and current, the edges of two ice floes crash together. With a cracking and deep, booming thunder, huge blocks of ice fissure, fracture, and lift into a mile-long, man-high ridge. But most of the energy — and most of the ice — is driven down into the sea. Hidden from human eyes, tons of interlocked whiteness form a deep keel in the darkness.

*A diver explores the black and blue world beneath the polar ice in this photo taken in 1974, the year in which Dr. Joseph MacInnis made the first dive into waters beneath the North Pole.*
*(Courtesy of Dr. Joseph MacInnis)*

Polar waters surrounding the Northwest Territories are among the world's most remote and least known. Their physical and chemical properties are concealed by distance, obscured by snow and cold, covered by thick layers of ice. They lie at the end of the earth — both geographically and scientifically — and remain even today relatively unexplored. Only in the last two decades have scientists been able to submerge in the Arctic Ocean, diving deep and staying down for significant periods.

Almost all of our understanding of these northern waters comes from nets, grabs, and coring and acoustic devices lowered into the ocean. Curious scientists have sounded and sampled, working from ships and ice stations as far north as the pole. But most North Americans still have a limited view of the polar ocean that stretches across the roof of their hemisphere.

To look up from inside this ocean is to see things differently. In springtime, when the sun is shining, it is a view of luminescent blue plates, smooth and broken, diamondlike, tinted with white. It is a scene of ice and icebergs, deep inverted blue and white towers, jutting hundreds of feet into cold darkness, sometimes touching the sea floor.

When icebergs stroke the bottom of the sea, they do so with ponderous, imposing energy — ripping, tearing and scraping deep-walled scars through the sediments, scars which can last for centuries.

Since 1970 I have explored more than 25 cold-water sites in the Northwest Territories. I have dived during all seasons — when the summer sun blazes 24 hours a day and when winter temperatures plummet to minus 50 degrees (minus 44 degrees C). At almost every location I discovered that life was scarce; the creatures I did see were generally small and colorless. There were, however, some notable exceptions: a river on Baffin Island trembling with hundreds of silver, swimming char; the Northwest Passage near Resolute swarming with curtains of green plankton; the intact wooden hull of the British ship *Breadalbane,* drowned since 1853, festooned with fiery red soft coral.

The *Breadalbane,* trapped in the ice in Victoria Strait and sunk while searching for Sir John Franklin's missing expedition, is the first of many ships to be discovered and explored beneath the waters of the Northwest Territories. Other ships — such as the *Investigator* and two of Franklin's ships, the *Erebus* and *Terror* — protected by depth and near-freezing water, defended by ice and darkness, will be almost as they were when they sank more than a century ago. If they fell beyond the range of down-reaching ice, their hulls, decks and cargoes will have changed little since they were abandoned.

It will take new technologies and substantial human perseverance to locate and explore these ice-covered ghost ships. But human beings are curious creatures. Computers, surface positioning devices, underwater imaging, and advanced diving systems will soon allow us unlimited access to the cold, deep waters.

Our undersea investigations will not be taken lightly. These dark waters are among the last unexplored corners of the world. After years of plundering the ocean, man is aware of the need for ocean preservation. Concern for the icy seas off the coast of the Northwest Territories — once taken for granted — is now part of our collective responsibility.

*In August 1980, Dr. Joseph MacInnis led the search team that located the remains of the* Breadalbane, *a three-masted English bark that sank in 1853. The most northerly shipwreck yet discovered, the* Breadalbane *lies south of Beechey Island in about 350 feet (105 meters) of water. (Painting of* Breadalbane *at Scott Polar Research Institute, Cambridge, England; photo courtesy of Dr. Joseph MacInnis)*

# The Long Trek

On Feb. 13, 1982, Will Steger set out from Baker Lake, Northwest Territories, on the trek of a lifetime — 18 months on the trail, covering 7,000 miles (11,300 kilometers) of wilderness stretching from northern Ellesmere Island to Alaska's Yukon Delta.

Accompanying Steger on various legs of the journey were his wife, Patti, friend Bob Mantell, and 10 Alaskan-Siberian crossbred sled dogs. The Stegers, who own and operate a winter survival school in Ely, Minnesota, spent two years planning the trip for which they designed and manufactured all of their equipment, blending traditional and modern materials and techniques.

*A narrow ledge on the Arctic Coast just west of the Mackenzie Delta was the scene of this mishap. Bob Mantell surveys the situation, trying to figure out how to right the 1,000-pound (450-kilogram) sled without the arduous task of unloading it.* (Will Steger)

**Above** — *Patti pours hot tea during a break on the trail between Great Slave Lake and the Mackenzie Delta. Trees along this part of the journey provided firewood and also offered protection from the harsh winds. During January, daytime temperatures remained around minus 40 degrees (minus 40 degrees C).* (Will Steger)

**Right** — *When the sea ice broke up in early July, Will and Patti cached their sled and winter equipment and continued with backpacks and dog packs. Here, Patti and five of the dogs ford the Lewis River, on northern Ellesmere Island, in mid-August.* (Will Steger)

**Left** — *Frost-shrouded trees line the banks of the Great Bear River, which flows between Great Bear Lake and the Mackenzie River. The river moves so swiftly that it remains open even at temperatures of minus 50 degrees (minus 44 degrees C), providing a source of moisture which condenses into a thick layer of frost on the surrounding trees. (Will Steger)*

*In the North, tidal action causes cracks, called leads, in the sea ice, which open and freeze over during the colder months. When the weather warms, the leads reopen and increase rapidly in width. Bob Mantell crossed a small lead on Greely Fiord **above** with little difficulty. The big lead shown at **right,** encountered in July, measured 50 feet (15 meters) across and had no ice bridges to cross. The problem was solved by tying together several chunks of ice to form a bridge. After the gear was transported, the dogs reluctantly followed. (Both by Will Steger)*

*An* inukshuk *stands on Rae Isthmus, at the base of Melville Peninsula. These man-shaped stone structures were built by the Inuit to serve as markers on their barren landscape. (Fred Bruemmer)*

# PREHISTORIC PEOPLES OF ARCTIC CANADA

*Editor's note: Robert McGhee is an archaeologist specializing in the prehistory of arctic Canada, and is presently employed by the Archaeological Survey of Canada.*

*By Dr. Robert McGhee*

Arctic Canada was the last major region of the habitable world to be occupied by human beings. By about 10,000 B.C., when mankind had spread from his tropical homelands to most regions of the earth, most of arctic Canada still lay beneath the glaciers of the last Ice Age. However, the glaciers were in retreat before a rapidly warming climate; great rivers of meltwater poured from their flanks, while icebergs calved into the arctic sea and the vast ice-dammed lakes to the south and west of the glaciers. Tundra vegetation spread rapidly over the mud and rocks left by the ice sheets, as seeds and spores were carried northward by wind, rivers and migrating birds. As the vegetation spread, so did the animals that lived from it — lemmings and ground squirrels, musk-oxen and caribou — and with them their predators — foxes and wolves, bears and man.

The first human inhabitants of the region were

Indian hunters who arrived from the south, almost certainly following the caribou herds which migrated northward each summer to calve and to feed on the lush tundra. By 6000 B.C., when only small, wasting remnants of the glaciers remained, Indians had established themselves as far north as Great Bear Lake, and eastward across the Barren Lands as far as Hudson Bay. Chipped-stone spearheads and other artifacts found in their campsites are similar to those used at the same time by buffalo hunters of the North American plains, and these northern hunters are thought of as a branch of the same Paleo-Indian culture. Their way of life was probably similar to that of the Chipewyan Indians of the Barren Lands, involving summer hunting on the tundra and a winter retreat to the shelter of the northern forest.

Far to the north, on the Arctic Coast and islands, conditions similar to those at present had probably become established by about 6000 B.C. The land was obviously habitable by human hunters, yet remained unoccupied for the following 4,000 years. When evidence of human occupation first occurs, about 2000 B.C., it shows the appearance of a totally new way of life, and one which almost certainly did not develop from earlier North American traditions. Both the characteristic forms of the newcomers' tent camps, with central hearth and midpassage of stone slabs, and the tiny chipped-stone tools found around their camps are similar to Siberian forms. It seems most likely that these first arctic people, known as Paleo-Eskimos, were recent immigrants from Siberia who arrived in North America only about 2000 B.C. By this time the Bering Land Bridge, by which earlier Indian immigrants had reached

These tiny stone tools were chipped by early Paleo-Eskimos from multicolored chert. The largest is only one and one-quarter inches (three centimeters) long. (Robert McGhee)

North America, had long been drowned beneath the rising waters of the Bering Sea. The Paleo-Eskimos most likely crossed Bering Strait on the treacherous winter ice, since there is no evidence that they possessed watercraft capable of an open-water crossing.

Within a few generations, these Paleo-Eskimos appear to have spread across most of arctic North America. Most of their campsites are small, the remains of occupation by one or a few families for a few days or weeks. In many areas they con-

*An Inuit woman from the Belcher Islands, in Hudson Bay, wears a garment made from eider duck skins. This type of clothing is no longer made. (Richard Harrington)*

33

centrated on hunting land animals; in other regions they hunted seals, but the numerous bones of fox and waterfowl in their camp remains suggest a heavy dependence on small game. With no evidence of the use of boats, nor of the float-harpoon gear so useful to later Eskimos in capturing sea mammals, their sea-hunting abilities may have been quite limited. Probably related to this limitation is the lack of evidence that they used oil-burning lamps. Without such lamps they could not have used winter snow houses, as even a small open fire of wood or blubber would have been too hot and smoky for use in a snow house.

Our impression of the way of life of the early Paleo-Eskimos is one of almost unbelievable meagerness, of tiny groups of people scattered over a vast landscape, living throughout the year in skin tents heated only occasionally by small fires of dwarf willow and animal bones. With relatively inadequate equipment for living in the Arctic, many local groups must have perished, yet the Paleo-Eskimos continued to occupy the region for more than 3,000 years. About halfway through this period, around 500 B.C., their way of life was transformed into what is known as the Dorset culture, marked by the appearance of oil lamps, winter house structures, larger settlements, and the appearance of a more prosperous and secure life. This change occurred during a period of cooling climate, which may have made sea-

*The remains of a Dorset winter village lie near the shore at Cape Storm, on the southern coast of Ellesmere Island. Vegetation has grown in the four shallow rectangular house pits and on dump areas in front. (Robert McGhee)*

hunting more productive for people adapted to hunting from the sea ice rather than from open water. If this interpretation is correct, it is an interesting contradiction to the general assumption that a colder climate makes arctic regions less productive for human occupants.

The Dorset people, continuing to live in apparent isolation from the rest of the northern world, developed a culture of unique fascination to archaeologists. Most fascinating is their art: tiny carvings of animal, human and spiritual beings, intimately and enigmatically related to their magical view of the world. The Dorset world, however, was to have a harsh ending. Around A.D. 1000, in a period of warming climate and reduced sea ice, their country was invaded from two directions. From the east came the Norse, who settled Greenland and explored the eastern coasts of arctic Canada. From the west came Thule Eskimos, descendants of Alaskan peoples who, during the preceding centuries, had developed the maritime hunting skills which were to make them the masters of all of arctic North America. Traveling in kayaks and large *umiaks,* capable of hunting sea mammals as large as bowhead whales, living in large winter villages of houses built from rock, whalebones and turf, and maintaining long-distance communication and trade by spring dog sled journeys, the Thule people rapidly overwhelmed their predecessors and occupied all regions of arctic Canada. They probably traded and fought as equals with the Greenlandic Norse, and within 500 years had occupied settlements abandoned by the vanished Norsemen.

Yet the Thule adaptation, efficient as it was,

*These small Dorset ivory carvings of bears were found on Bathurst Island. The collection includes two complete bears, a bear head, and a bear skull. The largest measures two and one-half inches (six centimeters) in length. (Robert McGhee)*

*The remains of this Thule winter village on Bathurst Island bristle with whalebones, evidence of the Thule's success as whalers. (Robert McGhee)*

**Above** — *The late Daniel Weetaluktuk, an Inuit archaeologist, stands beside a stone structure, probably Thule, on Devon Island. (Robert McGhee)*

**Right** — *Artist-ornithologist Roger Tory Peterson looks on as the oldest resident of Arctic Bay, on northern Baffin Island, demonstrates the use of an* ulu. *The half-moon-shaped knives have been used for centuries by Natives throughout the Arctic. (Richard Harrington)*

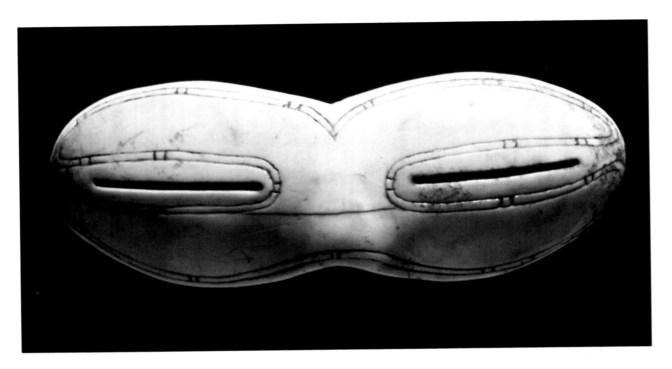

was in the long run not well suited to arctic Canada. With the cooling climate which set in after about A.D. 1200, and culminated in the Little Ice Age of about A.D. 1600 to 1850, increased sea ice blocked the movements of large sea mammals on which the Thule depended, and made open-water hunting less productive. In most regions, people adapted by either moving out or making greater use of land animals and small game. Some began spending the summers hunting in the interior rather than on the coast, and the permanent winter villages made possible by stores of summer-killed meat were abandoned. When European explorers began to penetrate the Canadian Arctic, they found a mosaic of Eskimo

*Simple decorative carving adorns these Thule ivory snow goggles, necessary protection against the glare of a snow-covered landscape. (Robert McGhee)*

groups doing their best to survive amid the deteriorating and confusing changes in their local environments.

Perhaps the most interesting lesson of arctic prehistory is that the Eskimo ways of life described by these explorers were not the result of adaptation to the arctic environment during several millennia, but were very recent phenomena: makeshift attempts to preserve what had recently been a way of life as rich and sophisticated as most in the nonagricultural world.

*The whalebone roof structure of this circular house was reconstructed by archaeologists, who are excavating this 900-hundred-year-old Thule village on Bathurst Island. (Robert McGhee)*

**Left** — *An Inuk, dressed warmly in caribou skin clothing, prepares to repair his igloo.*
*(Richard Harrington)*

**Below** — *An Inuk uses a saw to cut a block of soapstone, a popular medium for carving because of its availability and relative softness.*
*(Richard Harrington)*

**Left** — *An ancient fish trap remains in a stream near Tinney Hills, east of Bathurst Inlet. Stones were arranged to direct and concentrate the run of fish, which were then scooped up by Native fishermen. (Lyn Hancock)*

The crew of the HMS Terror, ill-clad for the arctic environment, pushes aside ice in an attempt to make a passageway for the ship. The Terror, under the command of George Back, was eventually frozen in and damaged.
(Metropolitan Toronto Library)

# Milestones In The History Of Northwest Territories

*Editor's note: Lyn Harrington has visited northern Canada several times, and has written many articles about her travels, as well as one book,* The Polar Regions *(1973). She lives in Toronto with her husband, writer-photographer Richard Harrington.*

*By Lyn Harrington*

The North is Canada's oldest and newest frontier. Discovery occurred in a series of bursts of exploration, carried out from Inuit skin boats and Viking longships to atomic submarines and giant aircraft, as new objectives and new techniques arose.

The first explorers sought alternate routes to China after Tartar hostility closed land routes. Columbus, looking for an approach from the east, discovered that the North American land mass blocked the way to the Pacific. The Dutch and English, seeking a northern route, sailed northeast, only to encounter impassable ice. This began the long search for the Northwest Passage; explorers sailed north between Greenland and Baffin Island, and west through Hudson Strait.

Then came exploration in the service of the fur trade. The Hudson's Bay Co. sent men north on foot to explore the Barren Lands and northern

*Samuel Hearne, born in London in 1745, joined the Royal Navy at the age of 12. In 1766 he entered the service of Hudson's Bay Co. and was stationed at Fort Prince of Wales on the Churchill River. Three years later the company sent him in search of a river reported by the Indians to flow through banks of copper. Accompanied by a group of Chipewyan Indians, Hearne reached the Coppermine River and followed it to its mouth on the Arctic Coast. This portrait of Hearne, reprinted courtesy of Cambridge University Library, was taken from the 1958 edition of Hearne's account of his travels:* A Journey From Prince of Wales's Fort in Hudson's Bay to the Northern Ocean. *(Courtesy of George Luste)*

forests; the Canadian partners of Montreal's Northwest Co. pushed discovery west to the Pacific and north to the polar sea.

The period from 1818 to 1862 witnessed great voyages and thousands of miles of coast surveyed for the first time. Naval gentlemen in the British Admiralty laid down regulations and instructions for men in frail wooden sailing vessels, but they had little conception of the difficulties confronting crews in damp ships sailing through ice fields or trudging blindly through uncharted wilderness. Captains and their men, inadequately clad, experienced starvation, cannibalism, mutiny, fear of the unknown, and the endless battle with cold, muskeg, or Natives unpredictably helpful or hostile.

The changeover from sail to steam marked a beginning of scientific discovery and a change of target. The search for Sir John Franklin's party resulted in more discovery than Franklin could have accomplished in two lifetimes. Attempts to locate a Northwest Passage were followed by the search for the North Pole; both objectives were reached early in this century. With the transfer of British claims in the North to Canada, the Canadian government began to take a deeper interest in the Northwest Territories, and the Geological Survey took steps to establish Canadian sovereignty of the Arctic Islands inherited from the British.

Then came awareness of the diversity of native peoples in the Canadian Arctic, with ethnological and biological expeditions crossing the Barren Lands. Transpolar flights shortened travel time between North America and Europe, and bush airplanes eased travel for trappers, prospectors

During the 1800s, mapping of the Canadian Arctic Coast was carried out piecemeal; separate expeditions each covered a small section of coastline. Dr. John Rae completed the project with his overland trek of 1846. Rae sailed from York Factory to Repulse Bay, from where he set out on foot, crossing Rae Isthmus to Committee Bay. He then surveyed the coastline from Lord Mayor Bay, at the base of Boothia Peninsula, to within 20 miles (30 kilometers) of Fury and Hecla Strait, at the tip of Melville Peninsula. This scene shows Rae's party landing at desolate Repulse Bay in late summer, 1846. *(Painting by Charles Comfort, courtesy of Hudson's Bay Co.)*

and government men, covering in minutes distances that required weeks on the ground.

Atomic submarines have traveled under arctic ice and surfaced at the North Pole. Floating ice islands provide space for scientific camps where men probe the jagged undersurface and the murky ocean floor for unsuspected navigational hazards, for old wrecks and new ridges.

Discovery still goes on.

# Discovery at a Glance

| | |
|---|---|
| **1000-:** | Norsemen from Greenland hunt on Baffin Island and the coast of Labrador. |
| **1497:** | John Cabot sails from England, sights the coast of Newfoundland, then ventures south. |
| **1500-02:** | Gaspar and Miguel Corte-Real sail from Portugal and land on the coasts of Labrador and Newfoundland. |
| **1509:** | Sebastian Cabot sails north along the coast of Labrador, enters Hudson Strait, and sights Hudson Bay, thinking it is the Pacific. By his own account, he continues north to 67 degrees before his frightened crew forces him to turn back. |
| **1576-78:** | Martin Frobisher makes three voyages to Baffin Island, claiming the discovery for Queen Elizabeth I. |
| **1585-87:** | John Davis discovers Davis Strait and explores part of Baffin coast and Labrador in three voyages. |
| **1610-11:** | Henry Hudson penetrates Hudson Strait |

*Martin Frobisher, born in England about 1539, began his career as a sailor at age 15. In 1576 he set out to find a northwest passage to the Indies, hoping to make his fortune. He made three voyages to Baffin Island, finding what he took to be gold in the bay which bears his name. The "fortune" turned out to be worthless pyrites.*
(Metropolitan Toronto Library)

and Hudson and James bays before his mutinous crew sets him adrift in a rowboat.

**1612-16:** Thomas Button, Robert Bylot, and William Baffin, on various expeditions, explore Hudson and Baffin bays as far as narrow Smith Sound and land at Jones Sound.

**1619-20:** Jens Munk is sent by King Christian IV of Denmark to find the Northwest Passage. Beset by early winter at Churchill, 62 men die of scurvy. Only Munk and two sailors survive to return home.

**1631-32:** Luke Foxe discovers Foxe Basin west of Baffin Island.

**1668-69:** Two Canadian fur traders, Pierre Radisson and Médard Chouart, known as Sieur des Groseilliers, persuade London businessmen to begin trading in Hudson Bay. The latter builds a successful fur trade post at Rupert's River, at the foot of James Bay.

**1670:** Because of the wealth of furs obtained, King Charles II makes his cousin Rupert governor of Rupert's Land — all the land drained by Hudson Bay — and grants a charter giving the Hudson's Bay Co. (HBC) exclusive trading rights.

**1690-92:** The HBC sends Henry Kelsey inland from York Factory to entice the Indians to bring their furs to the post on Hudson Bay.

**1715:** HBC sends William Stewart (Stuart) inland to make peace among the Indians and to explore land to the northwest. The first European to cross the Barren Lands, he probably reached Great Slave Lake.

**1719-21:** James Knight, 80, longtime employee of HBC, sets out to discover the mythical Strait of Anian, a direct route to the Orient, and to search for gold described by local Indians. All perish after the party's ships become trapped off Marble Island in Hudson Bay.

**1754-55:** Anthony Henday is sent inland by HBC; he crosses the prairies of southern Canada, and is the first white man to view the Canadian Rockies.

**1761:** Captain Christopher penetrates Chesterfield Inlet, the last hope for a southerly Northwest Passage.

**1769-72:** HBC at Churchill sends Samuel Hearne northwest across the Barren Lands to find copper desposits near the Arctic Ocean. After two unlucky starts, he succeeds in finding the Coppermine River, and brings back a sample of copper.

**1789:** Alexander Mackenzie of the Northwest Co. (NWC) follows a route from Montreal to Great Slave Lake, then takes a large river flowing north. The river is named for him, though he called it the River of Disappointment, for he hoped it would flow into the Pacific.

**1818:** Sir John Ross's first expedition. Sent by the British Admiralty in search of a Northwest Passage via Baffin Bay, he charts the west coast of Davis Strait and reaches Lancaster Sound, gateway to the passage, but sees it blocked by mountains — a mirage.

**1819-20:** William Edward Parry's first expedition. The British Admiralty offered prizes for westward exploration — up to 20,000 pounds for reaching the

In 1690 Hudson's Bay Co. sent Henry Kelsey on a trek inland to persuade the Indians to bring their furs to the Hudson's Bay Co. post at York Factory. He covered hundreds of miles of previously unexplored territory, and was the first white man to report on the buffalo and musk-oxen which roamed the prairie.
*(Painting by C.W. Jeffreys, courtesy of Hudson's Bay Co.)*

Pacific. Parry, sent by the Admiralty, threads through Lancaster Sound, Barrow Strait and Viscount Melville Sound, where he encounters the ice stream from Beaufort Sea. Winters on Melville Island, exploring it on foot, and wins prize of 5,000 pounds.

**1819-22:** John Franklin, on his first expedition, travels overland from York Factory to map the arctic coastline east of the Coppermine for the British navy. The party reaches Turnagain Point before turning back. Winter sets in and supplies run short — only Franklin and a handful of others survive the disastrous trek.

**1821:** Feuding between the two big fur companies, HBC and NWC, ceases when the two unite under the former's charter.

**1821-23:** William Edward Parry's second expedition. Sent by British Admiralty to discover the Northwest Passage via northern Hudson Bay, he puts in two winters, first at Winter Island, then near the entrance of Fury and Hecla Strait, at what is now Igloolik, and examines all shores.

**1824-25:** William Edward Parry, on his third expedition, explores Prince Regent Inlet west of Lancaster Sound, attempting to reach the Pacific. After an exceptionally early winter, one ship is crushed. Stores are stacked up on beach for future expeditions.

**1825-27:** John Franklin's second overland expedition. Five months' travel from New York brings the party to the mouth of the Mackenzie River, from where they map the coastline west to near Beechey Point, Alaska, and east to Coppermine.

**1829-33:** John Ross, accompanied by James Clark Ross, on his second expedition, makes first use of a steam engine in the Arctic. The *Victory,* their ornate paddle-wheel yacht, proves no match for ice-filled waters, and has to be abandoned in the Gulf of Boothia after three winters. After the fourth, the party sets out in small boats and eventually is rescued by a whaler in Lancaster Sound.

**1833-35:** George Back's first expedition tries to learn the fate of John Ross and the *Victory.* Back follows an overland route from Montreal, spending two winters at Fort Reliance at the east end of Great Slave Lake, where he learns of Ross's safe return to England. He goes on to descend the boulder-strewn Back River to Chantrey Inlet.

**1836-37:** George Back's second expedition, in the HMS *Terror,* is planned to complete the coastal survey west from narrow Fury and Hecla Strait to Turnagain Point. Instead the ship is trapped in the ice and damaged in the entrance to Frozen Strait. After 10 months the ship breaks free and eventually makes it back to Lough Swilly, Ireland, closest port for his badly damaged ship.

**1837-39:** Thomas Simpson and Peter Warren Dease are sent by HBC to descend the Mackenzie River and survey the arctic coastline, first to the west and then to the east. Simpson accurately boasts that he has found the Northwest Passage, since King William Land, previously believed to be a peninsula, proved to be an island, but he dies before he can report to the British navy.

**1845-48:** Sir John Franklin is sent by the British Admiralty to locate the Northwest Passage via Lancaster Sound and Barrow Strait. His ships *Erebus* and *Terror* become frozen in for two winters in Victoria Strait. Franklin dies, and his 129 men perish of scurvy, cold and hunger. At least 40 expeditions go in search of the party, resulting in widespread geographic discoveries.

**1846-47** Dr. John Rae's first expedition. He is sent by HBC to complete mapping of Thomas Simpson's farthest point east. Mainly on foot, Dr. Rae traces nearly all the coast of the Melville Peninsula.

**1847-49:** Dr. John Rae (second expedition) and Sir John Richardson conduct an overland search for Franklin west of Coppermine to the Mackenzie River.

**1848-49:** Sir James Clark Ross and Francis Leopold McClintock, caught in ice near the entrance of Prince Regent Inlet, sled around Somerset Island (separated from Boothia Peninsula by very narrow Bellot Strait) searching for Franklin's party.

**1850-54:** Robert McClure, approaching from the west on the *Investigator,* discovers McClure Strait between Banks and Melville islands, from which he can see the open water of Viscount Melville Sound. He has found a northwest passage, usually blocked by ice.

**1853-54:** Dr. John Rae, on his third expedition, is sent by HBC to survey the west coast of Boothia Peninsula by dog team. He meets Inuit who give him the first news of Franklin's party. Rae returns to England with the information to prevent wasted rescue attempts.

**1857-59:** Francis Leopold McClintock's second expedition, financed by Lady Franklin, travels down the west coast of Boothia Peninsula. Inuit give him definite information regarding the Franklin party and a stone cairn on King William Island yields the only written record ever found. Franklin had indeed found the strait discovered earlier by Thomas Simpson, which gives navigable access to wider waters beyond, but neither he nor his men realized they had found the devious and elusive Northwest Passage.

**1860-61:** Dr. Isaac Israel Hayes, firm believer in the theory of an open polar sea, attempts to sail to the North Pole. After his schooner *United States* is blown out of Smith Sound and damaged, he winters near Cape Alexander, on the west coast of Greenland. He foregoes plans to sail to the pole, and returns to Boston.

**1860-73:** Charles Francis Hall makes three expeditions to the eastern Arctic in search of Franklin relics. He finds evidence of Frobisher's party as well as Franklin's. Hall's final trip, in USS *Polaris,* is the first serious United States attempt to reach the North Pole. The disastrous voyage ends with Hall poisoned, the ship crushed, and one group of survivors adrift on an ice pan for six months before being rescued.

**1867:** By the British North America Act, three British North American provinces — Canada (then made up of Ontario and Quebec), New Brunswick and Nova Scotia — unite to form the Dominion of Canada.

*Between 1819 and 1825, William Edward Parry made three attempts to find the Northwest Passage. Although all were unsuccessful, he did find a true entrance to the passage, Fury and Hecla Strait. Parry was a skilled and innovative navigator — several of his recommendations to the British Admiralty, including suggested routes for future exploration and changes in equipment the ships carried, were implemented on later voyages.*
(Metropolitan Toronto Library)

**1869:** HBC sells Rupert's Land to the British government, which turns it over to the new Dominion of Canada the next year.

**1870:** Sovereignty over the arctic mainland is transferred to Canada. Province of Manitoba is enlarged from Northwest Territories (then called North-Western Territory).

**1875-76** The British Admiralty sends an expedition in HMS *Alert* to reach the North Pole. It reaches farther north than any previous ship on Ellesmere Island, wintering at Cape Sheridan (now Cape Union).

**1878-80:** Frederick Schwatka, young American lieutenant, travels overland from Chesterfield Inlet to King William Island in search for Franklin records reported by Inuit.

**1880:** Arctic Archipelago is transferred by Britain to the Canadian government.

**1881-84:** A U.S. Army expedition for first International Polar Year takes Lt. Adolphus Washington Greely to Lady Franklin Bay on Ellesmere Island to establish a meteorological station, carry out scientific experiments, and make sled journeys, which reach the farthest north point. Most of the party starve and only seven survive to be rescued.

**1893-1900:** Brothers Joseph B. and James Tyrrell, a geologist and a surveyor, make three expeditions, together and alone, for the Geological Survey of Canada and the Dominion Lands Survey. They travel on foot and by canoe to explore the (now) District of Keewatin.

**1898:** Yukon Territory is carved out of Northwest Territories (formerly called North-Western Territory).

**1898-1902:** Otto Sverdrup, a Norwegian, leads a private expedition to explore northern Greenland. Stopped by ice in Smith Sound, he meets Robert Peary attempting to reach the North Pole. Heavy ice persisting, Sverdrup crosses to Ellesmere and adjacent islands and makes major geographical discoveries. He claims the land for Norway, but this is not followed up. In 1930, the Canadian government pays Sverdrup $67,000 for expenses incurred and information gathered, and the Sverdrup Islands become unquestionably Canadian.

**1898-1902:** Robert Peary, in fourth Greenland expedition, attempts to reach the North Pole. Attains highest latitude to date north of Ellesmere, but men and dogs are in no shape for dash to pole.

**1898-1902:** David T. Hanbury, an American sportsman, makes three trips (one was abandoned) to explore interior Keewatin from Chesterfield Inlet to Coppermine River.

**1903-4:** A.P. Low is sent north by the Geological Survey of Canada to establish Canadian sovereignty over Hudson Bay and the Arctic Islands.

**1903-6:** Norwegian Roald Amundsen leads a private expedition in the first transit of the Northwest Passage entirely by sea, in the ship *Gjøa*.

**1905:** The provinces of Saskatchewan and

*In 1831, Sir John Ross was the first to determine the true position of the North Magnetic Pole, and marked it with the British flag, an event recorded by the expedition's artist. (Metropolitan Toronto Library)*

Alberta are carved out of the Northwest Territories from the 49th parallel to 60 degrees north.

**1905-6:** Robert Peary, on the second United States North Pole expedition, again reaches the highest latitude to date. Peary completes a survey of Ellesmere Island and reports sighting Crocker Land — a mirage — to the northwest.

**1907-9:** Dr. Frederick Cook, an American doctor with experience in the Antarctic, attempts to reach the North Pole in company of two Inuit. He claims to have reached his goal in 1908, but his achievement is still debated for a variety of reasons, including a lack of disinterested witnesses, failure to sight Meighen Island despite passing within five kilometers of it, and the fact that he reported his discovery to the King of Denmark.

**1908-9:** Robert Peary, in the third United States North Pole expedition, leaves Cape Columbia at tip of Ellesmere Island on March 1, 1909. Last support party turns back at 87 degrees 47 minutes. Peary, Matthew Henson (his manservant) and four Inuit dash to the pole on April 6, 1909. From Labrador, Peary telegraphs his claim to his New York sponsors, five days after news of Dr. Cook's claim.

**1908-12:** Vilhjalmur Stefansson and Rudolph M. Anderson head an expedition, sponsored by the Geological Survey of Canada and American Museum of Natural History, to study anthropology and biology in the northern Mackenzie and southern Franklin districts.

**1911-12:** George M. Douglas is sent to investigate Coppermine Mountains, via the Mackenzie River and then overland. He and fellow geologists find copper ore, but it is too distant for profitable mining.

**1913-17:** Donald B. Macmillan attempts to explore Crocker Land, sighted by Peary, but it proves to be merely a mirage. He carries out scientific observations in the Sverdrup Islands.

**1913-18:** Vilhjalmur Stefansson's second expedition. He and Rudolph M. Anderson are sent by the Canadian government to explore the western Canadian Arctic including Herschel Island. Their main vessel, the *Karluk,* is beset off Point Barrow and carried far west while Stefansson is ashore hunting. The ship is crushed in Siberian waters, and although most of the party manages to reach Wrangel Island, only 14 people survive the ordeal.

**1918:** By Order in Council of March 16, 1918, the North-Western Territory becomes the Northwest Territories, and is divided into three districts: Mackenzie, Franklin and Keewatin. This order takes effect Jan. 1, 1920.

**1921-24:** The Fifth Thule Expedition crosses northern Canada from Baffin Island to Alaska, completing the first traverse of the Northwest Passage by dog sled. Knud Rasmussen makes ethnological and archaeological studies of the Inuit.

*A few whalebones and fallen stone walls mark an ancient Thule occupation site on Ellesmere Island.*
*(Richard Harrington)*

Surface expression of ore bodies is commonly brilliant-hued gossan zones, formed by oxidation of metal-bearing minerals on the earth's surface. Many mineral resources in the Canadian Shield have yet to be discovered or evaluated. High transportation costs have prevented some ore bodies from being developed into mines. Mines in the Arctic generally extract high-profit ores such as gold, or lower-priced metals that are found in large deposits near a transportation route. Gossans shown in this photo (rust- and beige-colored areas in right center) are from an ore body near the Arctic Ocean that formed more than 2.7 billion years ago in an old volcano. (R. Michael Easton)

# GEOLOGY OF THE CANADIAN ARCTIC

*Editor's note: R. Michael Easton first became interested in geology in 1971 and has spent almost every summer since mapping rocks in the Northwest Territories. He earned his Ph.D. in geology in 1982 and now works for the Ontario Geological Survey. He is the author of approximately 45 geological books, articles and maps.*

*By Dr. R. Michael Easton*

The Canadian Arctic — Yukon Territory and Northwest Territories — is made up of a variety of geological terranes of various ages, from rock as old as 3.2 billion years to sands and gravels laid down yesterday. Much knowledge of the Canadian Arctic dates from the 1950s, when the Geological Survey of Canada undertook an ambitious, long-term helicopter mapping project of the region. In 1957, nearly 75 percent of Canada was still unmapped in a geological sense, and it wasn't until 1975 that Canada had been completely mapped at reconnaissance scales. (Generally, this means that one rock outcrop in a 10-square-kilometer area, about four square miles, has been examined.) These maps are adequate for determining the geological history of large regions in broad terms, but are not detailed enough for the evaluation of individual mineral prospects or mineral potential of a region.

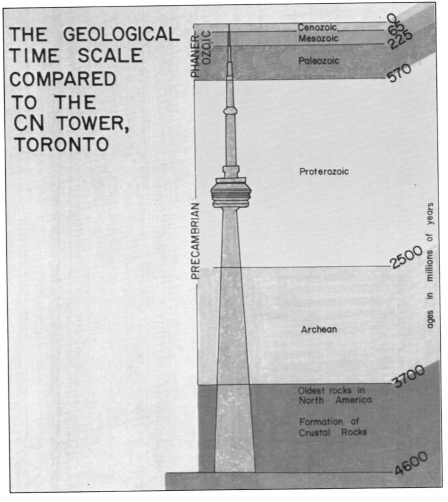

THE GEOLOGICAL
TIME SCALE
COMPARED
TO THE
CN TOWER,
TORONTO

*A comparison of the geological time scale with the Canadian National Tower in Toronto, which at 1,821 feet (555 meters) is slightly higher than the World Trade Center in New York, shows that most of the earth's history is represented by rocks of the Canadian Shield from the Proterozoic and Archean periods. (Reprinted with permission of Walter M. Tovell, Ontario Science Centre; courtesy of R. Michael Easton)*

Thus, knowledge of the geology of the Canadian Arctic, especially the ice-covered regions of the Arctic Islands, is still sketchy. Recent discoveries of petroleum and mineral resources in the Canadian Arctic help sustain an interest in the region, and encourage further geologic work for both scientific and exploration purposes.

The Canadian Arctic can be divided into a number of geologic regions, made up of geological provinces (areas of similar rock types, structure, origin and age) and orogens (areas of current or past mountain building).

The Canadian Arctic is underlain by rocks of five main geologic regions: Precambrian rocks of the Canadian Shield (3.2 to 0.6 billion years old); Paleozoic rocks of the Innuitian Orogen, or old mountain range (600 to 200 million years old); late Paleozoic and Mesozoic rocks of the Interior platform (450 to 200 million years old); and rocks of the Cordilleran Orogen in Yukon Territory and Alaska, representing the northern extension of the Rocky Mountains and the Coast Range of British Columbia (one billion years old to the present). A fifth region is made up of sediments of the continental shelf and the floor of the Arctic Ocean. Rocks of the Canadian Arctic span almost the complete range of earth's history; they also include almost every type of rock present on the earth's surface. Even kimberlites, the diamond-bearing rocks of South Africa, have been found in the Northwest Territories, on Somerset Island in the Arctic Islands. However, these deposits are not of commercial quality.

In general, the oldest rocks are present in the Canadian Shield in the Northwest Territories, and the youngest are found along the edges of North

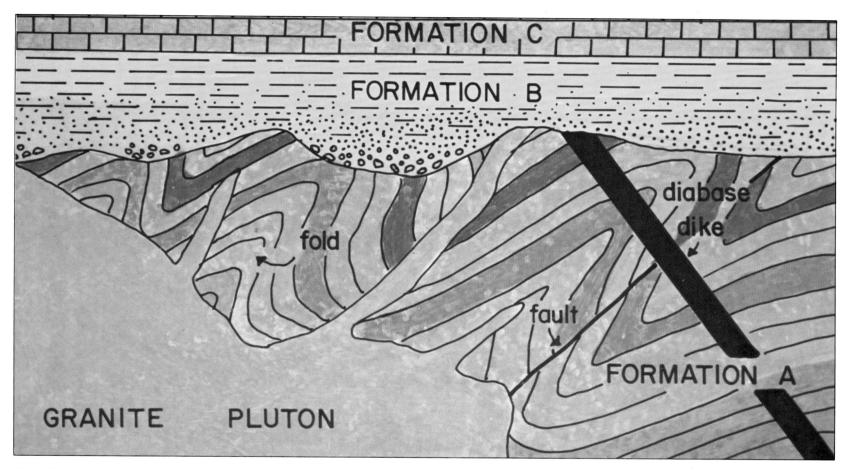

*This diagram shows how geologists determine the relative age of rock units and the geological history of an area. A sedimentary sequence, Formation A, was originally deposited horizontally. It was subsequently folded (warped), then faulted. Formation A was then intruded by a granite pluton and a diabase (granular, igneous rock) dike. The order of intrusion cannot be determined since the pluton and dike do not meet. Formation A, the granite, and the diabase were then eroded. Subsequently, Formation B was deposited on the eroded pluton and Formation A. This contact is an unconformity. Formation C was then deposited on top of Formation B.*
*(R. Michael Easton)*

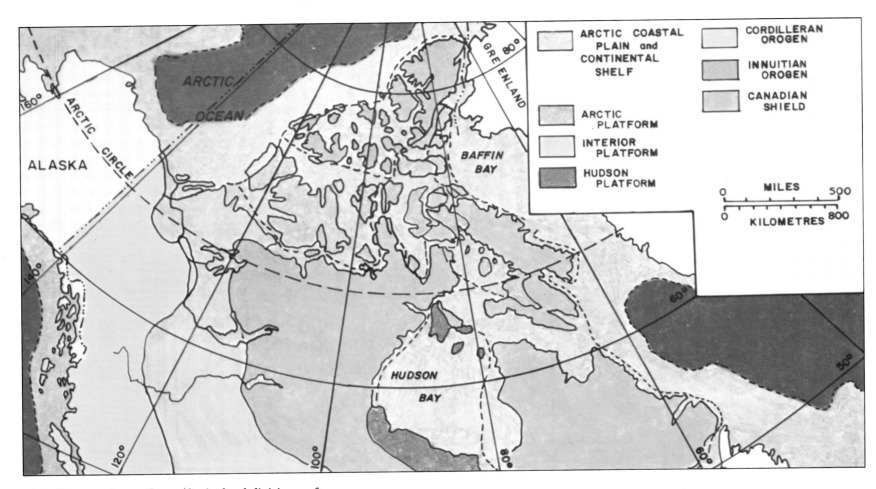

This diagram shows the geological subdivisions of
the Canadian Arctic. (R. Michael Easton)

*Pillow lavas are common volcanic rocks in much of the Canadian Shield. The pillowlike shape results from rapid chilling of hot lava (about 1,100 degrees) in sea water, forming a glassy rim (shown here by the hammer head) which allows the inner part of the pillow to cool slowly. The pillow lava in this photo was erupted from a volcano about 1.9 billion years ago.*
(R. Michael Easton)

*Unconformities, such as the one shown here, help geologists establish age relationships in rock units which have not been dated by radioactive decay methods. Here, a conglomerate in the upper part of the photo, composed of lithified sand and gravel, overlies an Archean age granodiorite pluton. Note how the conglomerate, laid down about 2.7 billion years ago, fills cracks in the older granite. The granite cooled and solidified about 3.2 billion years ago. The contact represents 500 million years of earth's history, the time from the appearance of the first hard-shelled fossils to the present.* (R. Michael Easton)

**Left** — *This iron-formation deposit consists of massive magnetite (iron oxide) ore (black) and calcium carbonate (brown), finely interlayered and contorted. Iron deposits in the Canadian Shield formed at two major periods of earth's history, about 2.7 billion and 2.2 billion years ago. Only a few small iron deposits have been formed since that time.* (R. Michael Easton)

America. Some geologists have suggested that this outward progression in age from older to younger is due to North America's outward growth from a much smaller nucleus of continental crust. Repeated periods of mountain building have attached other geologic terranes to North America, and with time, these regions have become stable parts of the continent.

Just as evolution is the unifying theory for biology, plate tectonics is the unifying theory for geology. According to this theory, the earth is divided into several large plates — North America is one such plate, the Pacific Basin another — which move over the earth's surface at rates of up to four inches (10 centimeters) a year, a small distance in our lifetime, but significant in geologic time. The boundaries of the plates are centers for volcanism, earthquakes, and mountain building. Geologists have found evidence of the oldest known plate movement, almost two billion years ago, in the Northwest Territories. As a result, we can attempt to understand the development of the earth in terms of processes currently acting on the earth's surface.

Because of the diversity of rocks in the Northwest Territories and the enormous time span represented by them, it is almost impossible to summarize the region's geology. Instead, I will highlight some of the more interesting features of the Precambrian, or Canadian, Shield, which makes up more than half of the Northwest Territories.

The Precambrian Shield is the backbone of the continent, literally and in terms of its mineral resources. The steel industry relies on iron ore supplied from mines in the southern reaches of the Canadian Shield. Similar resources are present in the Northwest Territories, but high transportation costs make mining these deposits uneconomical at present. Gold is one of the few commodities mined in the Northwest Territories, mainly because of its high market price. In the future, the mineral resources of the Precambrian Shield will almost certainly be exploited.

In Northwest Territories, rocks of the Canadian Shield, well exposed due to glaciation, have had a considerable influence on our understanding of earth's history. In addition to the evidence of ancient plates, some of the world's oldest fossils — stromatolites, a mixture of mud and algae — are found in the Northwest Territories. Also the glaciation of North America that took place between 20,000 and 10,000 years ago scraped clean the surface of the shield, laying bare its secrets, and scattering across its surface a variety of interesting glacial features such as drumlins and eskers. The glaciers also depressed the crust with their weight, and ancient shorelines, now high and dry, attest to the gradual postglacial uplift of the shield during the last 10,000 years. Glaciers formed the present landscape of the shield and exposed the rock of this backbone of the continent to the scrutiny of geologists. As a result, Canadians have developed considerable expertise in the science of geology, and have made notable contributions to our understanding of the earth.

The lure of riches — gold for Martin Frobisher, copper for Samuel Hearne, and oil today — brought man to the Canadian Arctic. In the future, geology will continue to be a significant factor in the development of the Northwest Territories.

*The pilot of a de Havilland Twin Otter aircraft on the Coppermine River prepares to drop off a geological mapping crew.*
*(R. Michael Easton)*

# Mineral Resources of the Northwest Territories

## By Gerry Wingenbach

*Editor's note: Gerry Wingenbach, a graduate of the University of Alberta, traveled extensively throughout Northwest Territories while working for the Canadian government. He currently works as a researcher and writer and lives in Vancouver, British Columbia.*

East of Canada's Yukon Territory, beyond the barrier created by the Richardson and Mackenzie mountains, stretches the vastness of the Northwest Territories. The scale is immense. Across muskeg, tundra and ice caps, the scattered settlements are home to only about 46,000 of Canada's 24 million people. Communities remain isolated, linked to the rest of the world by aircraft and satellite communications.

The North surged to significance during the cold war of the 1950s, when the North American Air Defense (NORAD) Command established a chain of Distant Early Warning radar stations — the DEW line. Prospectors also came, in search of gold, silver, lead, zinc, copper, nickel, iron and uranium. The present generation of Canadians has grown up believing that the future lies in the North, that the land and its resources could support millions of people. Yet the Northwest Territories still waits for expanded rail lines, capital investment and immigration. The Canadian government has yet to settle land claims with many groups of aboriginal people, which further complicates resource development.

Production and transportation of base metals remain relatively expensive. Labor costs are higher than anywhere else in Canada. Environmental concerns are also playing a role. In 1977 the federal government released the Berger Report on an extended inquiry into the construction of a pipeline through the Mackenzie Valley. The recommendation was a 10-year moratorium on construction.

Encouraged by Alaska's oil strike at Prudhoe Bay, industry and the Canadian government are funding major oil exploration projects in several areas of the Northwest Territories. Most of the exploration is centered around the Beaufort Sea, at the top end of the proposed Mackenzie Valley pipeline.

*This small piece of copper was found near Bloody Falls along the Coppermine River. (Richard Harrington)*

*A dredge builds an offshore island in the Beaufort Sea northwest of Tuktoyaktuk to support oil exploration. (Fred Bruemmer)*

*A drilling rig stands out in stark contrast to the tundra of the Mackenzie Delta north of Inuvik. Large gas deposits have been discovered in this region. (Fred Bruemmer)*

*The oil field at Norman Wells in western Northwest Territories produces more than a million barrels of crude oil per year. (Lyn Hancock)*

Interest in the petroleum potential of the Mackenzie region began with the earliest explorers. In 1789 Alexander Mackenzie observed oil seeps during his travels from Great Slave Lake to the Arctic Ocean. The first exploratory wells were drilled in the 1920s at the Norman Wells oil field on the north shore of the Mackenzie River. In 1942 the United States government, seeking a nearby source of fuel for its Alaskan troops, began construction of the Canol Pipeline to carry oil from the Norman Wells field to a refinery at Whitehorse, Yukon Territory. Although the pipeline served its wartime purpose, it later proved unnecessary and was dismantled and sold.

Today, the Norman Wells field produces more than a million barrels of crude oil per year and is the major supplier of fuel for communities to the north. The only other current producer of petroleum in Northwest Territories is the Pointed Mountain Gas Plant, about 18 miles (29 kilometers) northwest of Fort Liard, near the Yukon Territory border. The plant produced about 16 billion cubic feet (455 million cubic meters) of natural gas in 1981.

During the 1970s the Canadian Department of Energy, Mines and Resources ranked the Delta-Beaufort region a major petroleum province — "a great frontier that potentially contains major reserves of oil and gas." Most of the bounty is believed to lie offshore,

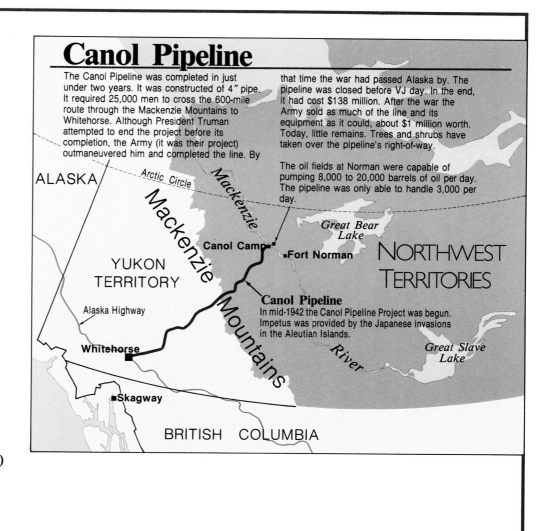

# Canol Pipeline

The Canol Pipeline was completed in just under two years. It was constructed of 4" pipe. It required 25,000 men to cross the 600-mile route through the Mackenzie Mountains to Whitehorse. Although President Truman attempted to end the project before its completion, the Army (it was their project) outmaneuvered him and completed the line. By that time the war had passed Alaska by. The pipeline was closed before VJ day. In the end, it had cost $138 million. After the war the Army sold as much of the line and its equipment as it could, about $1 million worth. Today, little remains. Trees and shrubs have taken over the pipeline's right-of-way.

The oil fields at Norman were capable of pumping 8,000 to 20,000 barrels of oil per day. The pipeline was only able to handle 3,000 per day.

**Canol Pipeline**
In mid-1942 the Canol Pipeline Project was begun. Impetus was provided by the Japanese invasions in the Aleutian Islands.

beneath the Beaufort Sea. Exploration is continuing, and petroleum is expected to be the region's major source of revenue well into the next century.

Most of the central part of the Northwest Territories is part of the Canadian Shield, where the main economic activity is mining. In the Great Slave Lake area, gold is the most common metal, widely distributed in a variety of rock. The largest deposits are associated with volcanic rocks on the north shore, near Yellowknife. Copper, lead, cobalt, nickel and silver are mined in the vicinity, and lead-zinc-cadmium production has been going on in Pine Point, near the south shore of the lake, since 1965. On the east shore of Great Bear Lake, significant quantities of silver are mined.

In the western part of the region, Tungsten, a small community on the Yukon Territory-Northwest Territories border, is the site of Canada's only tungsten-producing mine. Since the mine was built in 1962, production has been intermittent due to fluctuating prices and other factors. In 1981, the mine produced 3,500 tons (3,175 metric tons) of tungsten, valued at $40 million.

To the east, nickel-copper sulfide ores have been excavated at Rankin Inlet and Ferguson Lake. Low-grade iron deposits are present in the sedimentary sequences on Belcher and adjacent islands in Hudson Bay. Bands of iron formation are present in many areas, including narrow belts of metamorphosed volcanic and sedimentary rocks in northern District of Keewatin and on southern Baffin Island. Large high-grade hematite iron deposits are also found in sedimentary strata on Baffin Island.

The islands of the Arctic Archipelago, sparsely vegetated and nearly unpeopled, lie north of the Canadian mainland. The islands contain many small areas of Tertiary rocks, some bearing coal, which date back 65 million years. Within the archipelago, exploration focuses on petroleum. The Sabine Peninsula on Melville Island has gas reserves, but their full extent is not known. The Polaris lead-zinc mine — one of the world's most northerly metal mines — began operating on Little Cornwallis Island in 1981 and currently produces more than 2,350 tons (2,134 metric tons) per day.

Throughout the Northwest Territories the search for petroleum and minerals is continuing. Canadian Geological Survey reports leave no doubt that resources are present. The limiting factor to development is the relative high cost of extraction and transportation. Many mines and petroleum reserves remain in a nonproducing capacity, pawns to fluctuating world market prices.

*The tungsten mine near the Yukon Territory border operates both an open-pit (shown here) and an underground mine. (Richard Harrington)*

# Navigating the Northwest Passage

## By Capt. Thomas C. Pullen

***Editor's note:*** *Capt. Thomas C. Pullen, RCN (retired) was a government representative and advisor aboard the SS* Manhattan *during her historic voyage through the Northwest Passage in 1969. He is an authority on arctic navigation and ice breaking, and in April 1984 he received the Massey Medal for outstanding achievement in the exploration of the geography of Canada from the Royal Canadian Geographical Society.*

The Northwest Passage, the maze of ice-cluttered straits and sounds connecting Baffin Bay in the east to the Beaufort Sea in the west, has long been seen as the arctic key to linking the Atlantic and the Pacific oceans. The search for the elusive passage spurred nearly three centuries of exploration in the North. Today, in an energy hungry world, assured delivery of arctic oil and gas to world markets depends upon year-round navigation

*This pinnacled iceberg floats in Baffin Bay, considered the site of the world's largest concentration of icebergs. Scientists estimate that nearly 90 percent of the bulk of an iceberg remains under water. (Capt. Thomas C. Pullen)*

GREENLAND

Arctic Ocean

**Thule**

*Baffin Bay*

*Lancaster Sound*

Devon Island

Bathurst Island   Cornwallis Island

Melville Island   **Resolute**

Banks Island

**Barrow**

*Beaufort Sea*

**Sachs Harbour**

Somerset Island

Prince of Wales Island

Baffin Island

*Labrador Sea*

Arctic Circle

**Prudhoe Bay**

Herschel Island

*Prince of Wales Strait*

*Amundsen Gulf*

*Dolphin and Union Strait*

*Franklin Strait*

Boothia Peninsula

Victoria Island

*Coronation Gulf*

*Queen Maud Gulf*

King William Island

**Gjoa Haven**

ALASKA

Arctic Circle

NORTHWEST TERRITORIES

*Hudson Bay*

CANADA

# Transits of the Northwest Passage

**Halifax, Nova Scotia**

*Atlantic Ocean*

### Key to the travelers:
— SS *Manhattan* (1969)
— Franklin (1845-1848)
— Amundsen (1903-1906)

**Scale**
200 miles
200 kilometres

**Chester, Pennsylvania**

UNITED STATES

of the icy waterway. This can be accomplished only with special ships.

Most movement of ships in the North occurs during the summer — when the ice cover melts, breaks up or retreats, clearing a path for the vessels. Any ordinary ship attempting to remain in the Northwest Passage after the brief summer runs the risk of being trapped and becoming a part of the arctic scenery until breakup the following July.

Larger ships carry more cargo at a lower cost. In the Arctic this size-profit ratio pays an additional dividend: massive ships make excellent icebreakers. Success in breaking arctic ice is as much a matter of weight as it is one of power. Plans are being drawn for environmentally safe ice-breaking tankers — double-hulled ships with twin propulsion units — to transport petroleum. The inner hulls of these specialized ships would have strength greater than the single hulls of the standard tankers which carry oil across the oceans of the world.

*Canada's most powerful icebreaker, the* Louis S. St. Laurent, *cracks ice off Bylot Island in May 1970.* (Capt. Thomas C. Pullen)

**Left** — *The SS* Manhattan *makes her way north, cutting a path through the ice sheet on Baffin Bay in April 1970.* (Capt. Thomas C. Pullen)

**Right** — *The SS* Manhattan *is stopped by an old polar ice floe in Pond Inlet, off northeastern Baffin Island, in May 1970. The floe is 15 feet (five meters) thick and rock hard.* (Capt. Thomas C. Pullen)

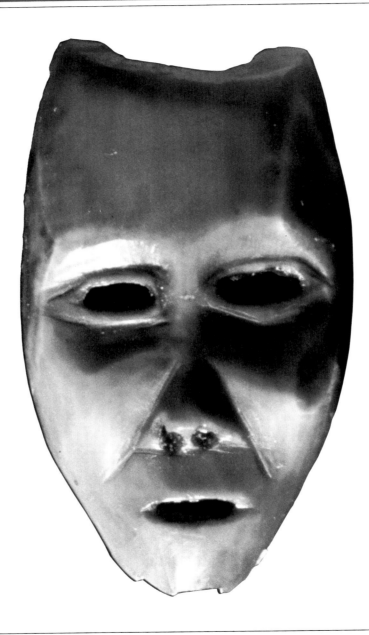

*This small ivory maskette shows the typical simplicity and deeply incised lines of early Dorset art.*
(Robert McGhee)

# ART OF THE INUIT

*Editor's note: George Swinton is a painter who has been collecting and studying Inuit art since 1957. He is the author of several books, including* The Sculpture of the Eskimo *(1972). He currently makes his home in southeastern Ontario.*

*By George Swinton*

Compared to Eskimos and Eskimoid peoples who have lived in the Canadian Arctic for more than 4,000 years, the true Inuit, the Canadian Eskimos of today, are relatively recent newcomers. They developed gradually during the last 400 to 500 years from Thule Eskimos who themselves had moved from Alaska east to the Mackenzie River only around A.D. 1000 to 1200. Yet, strangely enough, Inuit art seems to have a greater affinity with the art of the Dorset culture which preceded that of the Thule. This culture originated in the Hudson Bay region some 2,800 years ago and was able to sustain itself for almost 2,000 years. Therefore, it almost seems as if some contemporary ideas and styles in Inuit art had leapfrogged more than half a millennium.

While this may sound amazing and even unlikely, I am inclined to ascribe this phenomenon to several factors. In the first place, we must not

*This miniature Dorset ivory carving shows typical expressionism in its facial and body details. The tiny carving came from the Igloolik area and dates from A.D. 500 to 700. (Eskimo Museum, courtesy of George Swinton)*

forget the power of the oral traditions which were the major means of transmitting ideas, lifestyles, legends, taboos and rituals.

Secondly, but nearly equally important, were settlement patterns and economy: in contrast to the Thule people, the Dorsets and pre-World War II Inuit were nomadic caribou and sea mammal hunters who lived in nonpermanent hunting camps. The Thule lived in larger and more permanent settlements, built of heavy stones and whale ribs; and besides sea mammals and caribou, they hunted large whales that were sufficiently abundant in the Canadian Arctic Archipelago between A.D. 1000 and 1500.

Finally, there were climatic similarities during the phases of Dorset and Inuit cultures, although we are not certain as yet whether formal relationships between climate and art can or should be established.

Dorset and Thule art were vastly different. On the other hand, Dorset and contemporary Inuit art — despite dissimilar motivations — have several common features including style and, to some extent, content. Thule forms survived only rudimentarily into recent times and then mostly in wearing apparel and decoration. Aspects of magic-religious content of contemporary Inuit art can be traced back to Dorset forms and, perhaps, traditions.

Art of the Dorset period is characterized by

*Although less than eight inches (20 centimeters) long, this carved antler, found on Bathurst Island, is covered with approximately 60 faces. The strongly accented features and small size are characteristic of Dorset art. (Robert McGhee)*

starkness and almost complete absence of decoration. This contrasts directly with the richly decorated art and artifacts of contemporaneous Alaskan cultures and subsequent Thule art. Yet there exist spiritual similarities between Alaskan and Dorset art objects that derive from common Siberian roots, particularly evident in incisions of skeletal and joint mark motifs.

While there exist some graceful forms and smoothly polished surfaces in Dorset art, strength and power predominate in carvings small in dimension (one-half inch to four inches, or one to 10 centimeters, in height), but monumental in feeling. Thule art, on the other hand, does not possess this quality and remains small in size and scale. A Thule figurine, twice the size of a diminutive Dorset effigy, feels less powerful although its elegance and charm more than make up for its lack of strength. All Dorset figures, predominately male, have strongly accented faces; Thule figures, with few exceptions, are female and almost always faceless. Finally, Thule figures are often decorated, like their Alaskan ancestors, but Dorset human figures almost never are. Thule decoration is usually gently curved; Dorset decoration, if present, is straight and deeply incised.

In the historical period, no particular design traditions developed except that Thule-like figurines displayed an increasing sense of realism, lacking magic-religious content. At the same time, after arrival of explorers, missionaries, whalers and traders, a strongly representational style, still favored by most Inuit and southerners, started to evolve.

The beginning of the contemporary Inuit art phase can be dated to 1948-49. During these two

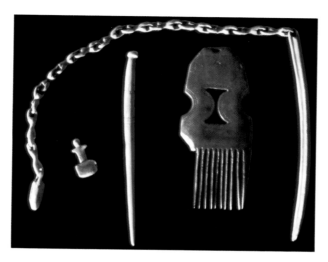

*An assortment of Thule ivory carvings, found on Cornwallis Island, includes a chain; tiny, featureless figurine; pin, and comb.* (Robert McGhee)

*A hunting scene — whaling from an* umiak *— was primitively carved on this Thule knife handle, found on Cornwallis Island.* (Robert McGhee)

*Inuit artists produce prints from carved stone blocks. At left, a woman rubs paper which has been placed over the inked block. The woman above carefully lifts the finished print (right) from the block. (All by Richard Harrington)*

years, the energetic efforts of James A. Houston, then a young Canadian artist, established "Eskimo Art" as a marketable commodity. Previous efforts by such agencies as the Moravian Brothers, the Hudson's Bay Co., and the Canadian Handicrafts Guild had always ended in failure. Houston succeeded, with the help of the latter two agencies and the Canadian government and, after starting out in Port Harrison (now Inoucdjouac or Inukjuak) and Povungnituk, both in Quebec, eventually covered the entire eastern Arctic.

Today, art activities stretch from Labrador in the east to the Mackenzie River in the west, and from Ellesmere Island in the north to Eskimo Point and Great Whale River in the south. And while the Inuit of Nouveau Quebec (the Ungava Peninsula) are not specifically part of the Northwest Territories, they are culturally and linguistically inseparable from the rest of the Canadian Inuit and are included in this article.

Part of the great success of this new art form is, in fact, its newness. This change in traditional art of the Canadian Eskimo has been difficult for some to accept. However, the Inuit have given up many of their old ways and still are in a state of transition. And that such people do produce new art forms is quite logical. But that they have done this so well is really a miracle.

This miracle is largely due to the Inuit's ability to fall back on their traditions and their perception of nature, reinforced by form-and-content

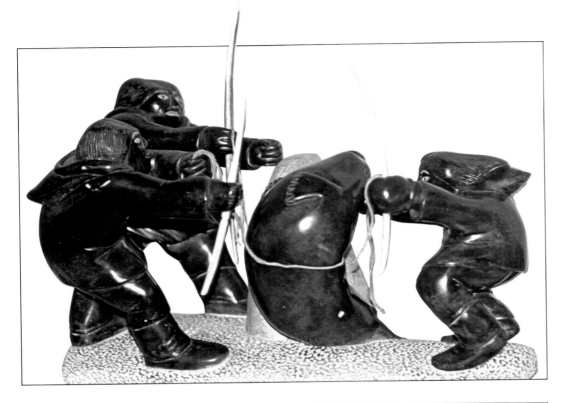

Contemporary Inuit soapstone carvers often use themes from their daily lives or the world around them. The carving above shows three hunters struggling with a seal on the ice; the hunter depicted at right has speared an arctic char. At far right, a polar bear displays the seal he has caught. (Above and right, Richard Harrington; far right, Fred Bruemmer)

*Artist Joseph Kaniak from Bay Chimo (Umingmaktok) demonstrates soapstone carving for visitors at Bathurst Inlet. (Lyn Hancock)*

echoes from Dorset culture. Yet, at the same time, because of its success, much art is produced today and vulgarization often obscures the authentic.

But genuine contemporary Inuit art is largely an affirmation of Inuitness: of dexterity with hands, of keen observation with eyes, of inventiveness with mind, of shrewdness with brain, of innocence yet candor with art. As one old Inuit friend said, they were "never always happy." But they knew how to laugh; and they still do. And their art reflects these qualities and lets us know what the Inuit feel and what they think about us, the non-Eskimos.

*This colorful Inuit wall hanging, by Marion Tuu'luq of Baker Lake, is an example of the way in which an artist pulls together complex, unrelated themes into a simple and harmonious design. (Wally Rice, courtesy of George Swinton)*

*This characteristic earthenware pot, by Donat Anawak of Rankin Inlet, was created as part of a short-lived pottery project in that community between 1963 and 1976. The pottery was often artistically magnificent, but the project proved economically impractical. (Wally Rice, courtesy of George Swinton)*

*Eskimo Point artist John Atok combines a stone carving of a hunter carrying home a caribou with the image of the oneness of man and animal that was so important to the Inuit's survival.*
*(Wally Rice, courtesy of George Swinton)*

Owls, a favorite subject for artists in the North, lend themselves well to carving and printmaking. Here, artist Simionie Kowjakuluk of Lake Harbour combines the two techniques, using three-dimensional form and very fine engraving of feathers to enrich the texture of the carved surface. *(Wally Rice, courtesy of George Swinton)*

*More than 10,000 musk-oxen roam the Northwest Territories mainland and Arctic Islands, a comeback for these shaggy mammals that were near extinction in the early 1900s. (Fred Bruemmer)*

# WILDLIFE

*Editor's note: Fred Bruemmer is a writer and photographer with a special interest in the North. For more than 20 years he has traveled extensively in the Canadian Arctic, Alaska, Greenland, Lapland, and Spitsbergen, and has written seven books and more than 500 magazine articles.*

*By Fred Bruemmer*

When James W. Tyrrell of the Geographical Survey of Canada crossed that vast central region of the Northwest Territories known as the Barren Grounds or Barren Lands in 1893, "of almost this entire territory less was known than of the remotest districts of 'Darkest Africa.'" In this remote wilderness he encountered caribou herds so enormous "they could only be reckoned in acres or square miles." Yet already then, Tyrrell noted, the musk-oxen of this region were becoming rare because of a "policy of systematic slaughter in quest of the princely robes so much in demand by the fur traders." Between 1862 and 1916, the Hudson's Bay Co. alone bought 15,000 musk-ox skins. They were made into superb sled blankets.

Explorers were often enthralled by the wildlife wealth of the Far North. At other times, they were appalled by the barrenness of the region.

*A batch of arctic char lies frozen on the ice of Lake Hazen, the most northerly lake on the continent. (Mary Meredith)*

The American Charles Francis Hall, visiting the head of Baffin Island's Frobisher Bay in 1861, was amazed to see hundreds of seals; the "water and the air were black" with eider ducks; and the rivers were teeming with char. "Indeed we are in a land and by rivers of plenty," he wrote. A few years later, the English traveler Warburton Pike crossed the far northern tundra in winter and was haunted by its impression of utter desolation, a land seemingly devoid of all life: "A monotonous snow-covered waste. A deathly silence hangs over all. . . .the awful spell of solitude."

Such disparate descriptions are hardly surprising. Many northern animals are migratory. They tend to bunch and follow ancient routes and anyone who sees such a mass migration, be it of caribou or snow geese or sandhill cranes, cannot fail to be deeply impressed by such a profusion of life. It is then easy to forget that one sees the gathered animals of an immense region.

Other northern animals are cyclic, rare in some years, incredibly abundant in others. Snowshoe hare populations wax and wane in a roughly 10-year rhythm, and the population of the lynx, its main predator, rises and crashes in synchronization. Snowshoe hares are stunningly fecund. Females bear as many as 10 young per litter, and the hare population can increase a hundredfold in just five years. Finally the overbrowsed plants fight back. They develop toxins that act as hare repellents. Deprived of food, the superabundant hares starve to death, populations dwindle, plants recover, lose their toxins and provide food for the remaining hares, and the 10-year cycle begins anew.

Lemmings, too, are cyclic. One year they are rare, with less than one pair per acre of tundra. The following year they are more numerous and visible. The third year, lemmings are everywhere, and the fourth year, at the peak of their cycle, the tundra is aswarm with these small rodents. Peak years are feast years for the many predators that rely partially or primarily upon lemmings. The female snowy owl, hormonally stimulated by the sight of so much food, lays an extra-large clutch of eggs, and the pair may succeed in raising all their ever-hungry owlets. Jaegers, gull-like birds with hawklike habits which, in poor lemming years, may not breed at all, now raise without difficulty two young per pair.

Arctic foxes have large litters, and Inuit trappers have a bountiful winter season. Wolves eat mainly the abundant and easy-to-catch

*Caribou thunder across the shallow part of a lake in Northwest Territories. Hundreds of thousands of these descendents from the Miocene period (about 20 million years ago) roam the Northwest Territories mainland. In the Arctic Islands to the north, a much smaller herd of Peary caribou are declining from pressure by hunters, industrial development, and an exceptionally harsh climate. (Fred Bruemmer)*

*Basis for much of the food chain of the Arctic's wildlife, lemming populations at times number in the hundreds of thousands and at other times border on scarcity. In summer the lemming's coat blends with the tundra; in winter, with the frozen snow. (Both by Fred Bruemmer)*

lemmings, and more caribou calves survive. In such years, even placid, herbivorous caribou slay lemmings with their broad hoofs and eat them, tiny tidbits of protein and fat and salts.

The two great biomes of the Northwest Territories are the boreal forest, the dark, primarily coniferous forest of the North and, beyond it, the tundra. The tree line, the forest's northern limit, is a great divide. The black bear is fairly common in some of the forested regions. The red squirrel and its main predator, the marten; the spruce grouse; gray jay; and many other species venture to the forest edge but not beyond. Others, the ptarmigan and its main predator, the gyrfalcon; the snowy owl; the arctic fox; and the musk-ox are creatures of the open tundra. Barren Ground grizzlies inhabit a relatively small area along the northwestern coast. A few animals, like the wolverine, are equally at home in the northern forest and upon the tundra. And the caribou commute, spending summer upon the tundra and winter within the forest belt.

The division of species can be quite abrupt. Just south of the tree line, about 10,000 species of insects exist in the boreal forest. A few miles farther north, on the tundra, only 500 insect species are found.

This paucity of species in the Far North reflects the harshness of the Arctic, and the specialization required to prosper in a land where climatic conditions are so inimical and food sparse. Less than 40 land mammal species are found in the Northwest Territories. Bird species are much more numerous and varied, but most are fair weather visitors. They come to the North in spring or early summer, when the weather is relatively clement and food is plentiful, and they depart with their offspring before winter's icy embrace enfolds land and sea. Of the roughly 120 bird species that breed in the North, about 11 species are year-round residents north of the tree line: willow and rock ptarmigan, ravens, snowy owls, two species of gulls, some hoary redpolls, gyrfalcons, black guillemots, and a few common and king eiders.

Most arctic birds are migrants, and many make annual flights between northern breeding grounds and wintering areas that are miracles of endurance and precise navigation. Knots are handsome, stocky shorebirds that breed in the Far North. Those from Baffin and Ellesmere islands fly east in fall, cross the vastness of Greenland's icecap and winter on the shores of Britain and Holland. Knots that breed in the central and western part of the Northwest Territories take a totally different route, south to winter on the coast of Argentina. Many fly to the end of the Americas at Tierra del Fuego. Perky, sparrow-sized wheatears of the eastern Arctic winter in west Africa, and beautiful lesser golden-plovers of the summer tundra head for the pampas of Argentina.

Champion migrant of all birds is the arctic tern. This delicate, four-ounce (110-gram) bird commutes yearly and seemingly without effort between the ends of the earth. It nests along arctic shores as far north as there is land and flies south in fall as far as Antarctica. Some banded arctic terns are known to have lived for more than 30 years. In their lifetime, these dainty birds will have flown more than a million miles.

The stay-at-homes, land mammals and the few bird species that do not migrate, must cope with winter's cold and darkness. Most eat voraciously

*Performing the duties of cleanup crew, these arctic foxes seek tidbits left by their larger northern neighbors, polar bears.* (Fred Bruemmer)

during summer's brief feast to amass fat reserves for the long, lean winter. And all winter dwellers are superbly insulated by fur, fat or feathers. The mighty musk-ox has small, densely furred ears, short stocky limbs, a massive, compact body, and a four-inch tail. Its huge cloak of coarse guard hair hangs nearly to the ground and beneath it the musk-ox has a thick layer of extremely fine, dense underwool. Thus shielded from the cold, musk-ox can endure, with little loss of body heat, temperatures of minus 40 degrees or minus 50

**Left** — *Established in 1922, Wood Buffalo National Park, on the border of Northwest Territories and Alberta, is home to about 5,000 bison. The park was originally set aside to ensure survival of the last herd of wood buffalo; later plains bison were brought in from other parts of Canada and today all the bison in the park may be hybrids.*
*(Richard Harrington)*

**Right** — *A female polar bear and her two cubs patrol a shoreline in the High Arctic. In the eastern Arctic, a polar bear does not breed until it is four years old, and a female can bear young only once every three years at most. Polar bears generally live 10 to 15 years, but they can live longer. (Fred Bruemmer)*

*Snowy owls, such as this youngster photographed at Cape Parry at the tip of Parry Peninsula, nest in dry areas of the tundra and depend upon lemmings as their primary food.*
*(Fred Bruemmer)*

**Above** — *A black guillemot carries fish to its young at a nest on a tiny island in northern Hudson Bay. These seabirds are rare in the western Arctic with only one small colony on Herschel Island in Yukon Territory. They are common along eastern arctic coasts from Ellesmere Island to Labrador and Hudson Bay.*
(Fred Bruemmer)

**Right** — *An ivory gull stands guard over its chick at a nest on Ellesmere Island. Until the late 1970s, only one ivory gull colony was known in the Canadian North. Since then, seven others have been discovered, most of them in the interior of Ellesmere Island, on nunatak cliffs surrounded by glaciers or ice fields.* (Fred Bruemmer)

degrees (minus 40 degrees or minus 45 degrees C) and storms of 60 mph.

Polar bears are equally well protected. Polar bear hair is filled with air chambers. The hair is oily and sheds water. And the bear's whitish hair can transmit solar energy, including that in the ultraviolet range, to the animal's black skin where it is absorbed as heat.

Arctic ground squirrels avoid the rigors of winter by hibernating. The squirrels stuff themselves so persistently all summer, they often more than double their weight. Swathed in fat, they retire in fall from the hostile upper earth to

**Above** — *Hooded seals, like this mother and pup, are distributed in the Gulf of Saint Lawrence and in the Atlantic east and north of Newfoundland in winter and spring; in summer these seals move into Davis Strait and Baffin Bay and range as far north as the coast of Ellesmere Island.*
*(Fred Bruemmer)*

**Right** — *A harp seal checks the surrounding ice for danger. In winter and spring, this species ranges along the north Atlantic coast; in summer, however, the seals swim into Hudson Bay and into waterways surrounding the Arctic Islands.*
*(Fred Bruemmer)*

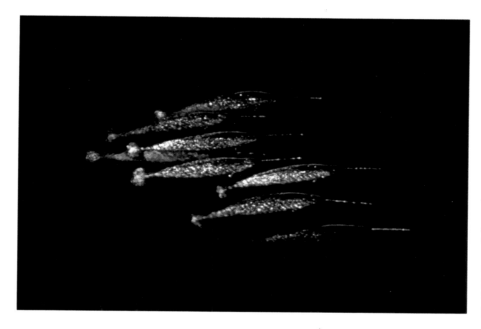

*Resembling speckled torpedoes pushing spears, a pod of narwhals swims along the Arctic Coast. Usually only male narwhals have the single tusk which gives these animals the nickname, sea unicorn. (Fred Bruemmer)*

*Swimming with its head out of water, a beluga whale and its pod mates course waters of the Northwest Territories. Belugas range along the coast of the Canadian Arctic, into Hudson Bay, and south to the Gulf of Saint Lawrence. A few sightings have been reported off Cape Cod and one off the coast of New Jersey. (Fred Bruemmer)*

special hibernation chambers, munch stored food for about a month, then sleep soundly for the next seven months.

Lemmings are too small to be cloaked in fat. Snow is their winter blanket. They build their globular grass nests beneath thick snow in the lee of hills and ridges. The temperature beneath snow three feet (one meter) thick can be 70 degrees (40 degrees C) warmer than the air temperature above it, and lemmings dig long runways to reach the surrounding vegetation.

While wool, which protects most land mammals from winter's lethal cold, is a superb insulator, the down of birds is even better. It traps body-warmed air near the bird's skin, and hard contour feathers surround the bird like a windproof shield. Some birds, like ptarmigan, also have densely feathered feet. These squat winter residents often burrow into snow to sleep, protected by the snow from cold and enemies.

Most arctic animals are superbly adapted to the harshness of nature. Man has been and still is their principal enemy. Commercial exploitation and overhunting have reduced many species. Some, like the musk-ox, have recovered thanks to prolonged protection. Bowhead whales were pursued so ruthlessly that even now, more than 50 years since commercial whaling ceased, they still are extremely rare. Caribou are severely reduced from former numbers in large parts of their range. In coming decades, as mineral exploration and exploitation proceed apace in the North, much caution and research will be required to safeguard the wildlife of the Northwest Territories.

# Subsistence

Hardy residents of Canada's High Arctic depend upon the land and sea for sustenance. In times of plenty, the rich life of the land and sea offers a wide range of nourishment: meat, fish, birds, berries and greens for food; skins and bark for clothing; bones and shells for utensils. But the land doesn't always provide, and there are times of scarcity which, in years past, brought untold hardship.

Let's meet some of Northwest Territories' many residents who live by subsistence.

**Right** — *Jeffrey Jackson, 18, son of Wilfred and Lucie Jackson of Fort Good Hope in western Northwest Territories, builds a wolverine trap in the foothills of the Mackenzie Mountains.*
(John Goddard)

**Far right** — *Arctic char hang to dry at this summer camp near Bathurst Inlet in the High Arctic.*
(Fred Bruemmer)

The Inuit community of Baker Lake, population about 1,000, on the shores of a lake with the same name, lies about 170 miles (280 kilometers) west of Hudson Bay. The village is unique as an inland, rather than coastal, Inuit settlement. While game near town is scarce, Inuit families set up hunting camps in the nearby Barren Lands, their ancestral homeland. This Inuit family has camped about 15 miles (24 kilometers) from Baker Lake.
*(George Luste)*

Andy Awa hunts Barren Land caribou along the shore of Baffin Island. *(Robert Semeniuk)*

Mrs. Johnnie Klondike scrapes a moose hide at Jean Marie River along the Mackenzie River. *(Lyn Hancock)*

**Left** — *A young Inuk stands guard over a kettle of eider eggs on southern Baffin Island.*
(Fred Bruemmer)

**Below** — *Bertha Ruben of Paulatuk displays her skill at muskrat skinning, just one of the skills required for subsistence living. Bertha has won the Good Woman contest at the Northern Games more often than any other contestant. Typical Good Woman events include fire lighting, tea boiling, bannock making, and duck plucking.*
(Lyn Hancock)

*Gardeners harvest some of the produce from Edwin Lindberg's garden along the Blackstone River between Fort Liard and Fort Simpson in western Northwest Territories. (Lyn Hancock)*

*In the summer, Inuit hunt harp seals along the east coast of Baffin Island. This harp seal has been shot and must be quickly harpooned before it sinks. Seals shot in summer sink faster than those shot in winter because there is less fat on their bodies in summer.*
*(Robert Semeniuk)*

Inuit from Baffin Island hunt ringed seals on the spring ice of Foxe Basin. The hunting party waits at the seal's breathing holes (left). When a ringed seal surfaces, it is harpooned (above).
(Both by Robert Semeniuk)

*Seals contribute meat and hides to the subsistence larder of the Far North. This Inuit woman is scraping a sealskin that has been stretched and staked to dry at Lake Harbour.* (Fred Bruemmer)

**Above** — *Paulosie Ataguttalukuttuk inflates an* avataq, *or sealskin float, to be used as a harpoon buoy.* (Robert Semeniuk)

**Right** — *A father teaches his son how to throw a harpoon on the ice floes of Foxe Basin, west of Baffin Island.* (Robert Semeniuk)

**Left** — *An Inuit trapper brings home an arctic fox from his trapping area near Repulse Bay. Pelts from these animals are sold to fur buyers and used to make clothing and household items.*
(Fred Bruemmer)

**Below** — *Villagers at Tuktoyaktuk butcher a beluga whale.* (Lyn Hancock)

*Mary Tapana, oldest woman at Bathurst Inlet before her death in 1983, shows off some of the arctic char she used to feed her family. Even at the time of her death, Mary was subsisting almost entirely off the land, eating fish, caribou and seal.* (Lyn Hancock)

*Having cut through ice several feet thick, this fisherman jigs for more fish to add to his catch of two fine lake trout.* (Fred Bruemmer)

*A fisherman jigs with a line and lure at Repulse Bay. The leister beside him is used for spearing fish.* (Fred Bruemmer)

*Government, mining, transportation and communications, and tourism form the mainstay of the economy of Yellowknife, population about 10,000, capital of Northwest Territories. In 1984 the town celebrated its golden anniversary.*
*(Richard Harrington)*

# TODAY

*Editor's note: John Goddard is a former reporter for The Canadian Press (CP) wire service who established CP's first permanent Northern Bureau, based in Yellowknife, in 1982. He currently works as a free-lance writer.*

*By John Goddard*

They are called "the Walkers." Their chief purpose in life is to shuffle among the pastel-colored bungalows of Rankin Inlet on the western shore of Hudson Bay. Occasionally they venture to the end of the cove where old people keep tents and fishing gear. Or they stroll up the hill opposite, to the satellite dish, to look across the rolling tundra that continues inland for hundreds of miles.

Sometimes the Walkers ride: in winter, furiously over the sea in snowmobiles; in summer, madly over the airport road in three-wheeled buggies, tossing up storms of dust. Sometimes the Walkers loiter. They finger the rock albums at the Hudson's Bay Co. store, watch TV at Ollie's sandwich bar, play video games at Yvo Airut's arcade, or hang out at the shacklike hamburger shop everyone calls The Fast Food, though customers go there to kill time, not save it.

The Walkers are Inuit teenagers and young adults who have lost the skills needed to live off the land and who have dropped out of school too early to get good jobs. "Boring" is their favorite adjective.

"Boring, eh?" says Michael Aklunark, 18, a regular at The Fast Food and a typical Walker. "I finished grade eight three years ago. Now I work sometimes for the Housing Corporation." The local school goes to grade nine but he sees no point in finishing. The nearest high school is in Frobisher Bay, 800 miles (1,290 kilometers)

east — one of only seven high schools in the Northwest Territories counting those in Yellowknife and Inuvik. Parents in Rankin Inlet, population about 1,000, generally dislike sending their children so far from home and many share a low regard for book-learning anyway. So Aklunark stays in Rankin. Sometimes he substitutes for a friend at the Housing Corporation when the friend wants a couple of weeks off. Sometimes Aklunark goes seal hunting with a few buddies, which is fun, he says: "If the seals don't come, we ride around in the boat instead."

The nickname "Walkers" is unique to Rankin Inlet, but the phenomenon is widespread. Aimless youths fritter away their lives in every Inuit and Dene settlement across the Northwest Territories. They are a walking symbol of the disruption northern native peoples are undergoing. Their search for a meaningful future is of paramount concern in every northern settlement.

For millenia, idleness was a luxury few Northerners could afford without risk of freezing and starving. Life became marginally easier in some respects when European whalers and fur traders appeared, introducing rifles, flour and tea. Native people changed their ways of life to accommodate the fur trade, which began in the early 1800s in the Mackenzie Valley and at the beginning of this century in the eastern Arctic. Life began to revolve around trading posts and to a large extent northern Natives came to depend on fur sales for their livelihood. But essentially the native peoples were still living traditional lives on the land — in the forests in the case of Dene, on the tundra and sea ice in the case of Inuit. Profound changes began to take place only recently. When fur prices

*Michael Aklunark (left) and friend Daniel Kadlak, both of Rankin Inlet, enjoy a break at The Fast Food. (John Goddard)*

114

The old and new blend in the lives of today's Inuit. A snow machine and sled help these hunters get their caribou (left); a traditional dog team, harnessed in fan formation, pulls travelers across Cumberland Sound. *(Left, Fred Bruemmer; below, Richard Harrington)*

fell in the 1950s, the federal government moved in to distribute welfare, establish schools, and build houses. For the first time, native people moved into settlements. Families were still drifting in off the land 15 years ago, which means today's Walkers either were born in hunting camps or are first-generation townfolk.

Settlements now characterize life in the Northwest Territories. There are 60 of them sprinkled thinly across one-third of the Canadian land mass. Dene and Metis peoples occupy the Mackenzie River drainage system in the west; Inuit live in the Arctic, east and north of the Mackenzie Basin beyond the tree line. Of course white people live in the North too. Forty-two percent of Northwest Territories' 46,000 people are non-native — a sizable group. But their importance is diminished by several factors. Most were born outside the Northwest Territories, most came north for two- or three-year terms, and few intend to retire in the North. Some live in settlements, but most are concentrated in the Northwest Territories' five towns, living much as they would in southern Canada: in Yellowknife (the capital, population about 10,000), Hay River (population 3,322) and Fort Smith (population 2,265) in the southwest; Inuvik (population about 3,000) in the northwest; and Frobisher Bay (population 2,444) in the southeast. The permanent population is predominantly Native — nearly 60 percent of the total — and most native people live in settlements.

Settlements differ in size, setting and atmosphere. Fort Norman (population 332), where elderly Dene women smoke moose skins in tepees overlooking the Mackenzie River, appears to have little in common with Grise Fiord (population 91)

in the High Arctic, where Inuit hunters sit on their doorsteps in July firing at seals swimming in to feed. Coppermine on the central arctic coast (population about 800) positively bustles compared to Sachs Harbour (population 142) dotting the shore of Banks Island.

But settlements are alike in the way they function. A family toilet is almost invariably a can fitted with a seat and garbage bag. Running water is not common. A water truck makes the rounds once or twice a week to fill a barrel or tank in each home. The typical house is a prefabricated, government-built, oblong bungalow rented

*Colorful clothing adorns these residents of Grise Fiord, population 91, near the southern tip of Ellesmere Island. (Mary Meredith)*

*Now known as Tuk and formerly called Port Brabant, Tuktoyaktuk, population about 800, lies on the Arctic Ocean near the mouth of the Mackenzie River and is the base for oil exploration in the Beaufort Sea. (Fred Bruemmer)*

Celebrants at the Beavertail Jamboree spring festival in Fort Simpson, population about 1,000, gingerly tip a huge cake on its side to get through the door of the community hall. *(John Goddard)*

*Aiming for the seal ornament dangling from the pole, this contestant participates in the one-legged kick at the Northern Games in Inuvik. The games are contests held at different places in the North each year. Eskimos and Indians come to the gatherings to show their skill at games, songs and dances, crafts, and traditional skills.*
*(Lyn Hancock)*

*The women of Igloolik put all their effort into this tug-of-war during a spring festival.* (Fred Bruemmer)

*Commissioner John Parker, head of the government for the Northwest Territories, visits Fort McPherson in far western reaches of his jurisdiction.* (John Goddard)

mercial char fishing have developed in some settlements. But most places have no economic base. The few jobs available are such tasks as driving the (government) water truck or putting up (government) houses.

The choice real estate in each settlement has usually gone to the missions, the Mounties, and the Hudson's Bay Co. They got there first. But newcomers make up the elite: teachers, nurses, the wildlife officer, and top-level government administrators. They have flush toilets. Their houses are better than most. On good salaries and generous living subsidies, they maintain a middle-class life. Most stay two or three years before returning "home."

For native residents, the settlements are not truly "home" either. Almost all live to some extent on the land. Fort McPherson (population 781) and Aklavik (population 800) in the Mackenzie Delta turn to ghost towns in the muskrat-hunting season. Many families spend more time in camp than in town. The Idlouts, an Inuit family, quit town entirely several years ago to resume camp life on Somerset Island. Other families, tied to steady jobs, get out on weekends to hunt. Even the Walkers, despite their penchant for video games and french fries, still thrill to a caribou chase and a night under the stars.

Native northerners live in two worlds: on the land and in town. An Inuit hunter might stalk seals in the morning and be back at night to watch "Hockey Night" in Canada via satellite. This might seem a happy way to divide one's time. But change has come too abruptly. The native psyche is split between the Stone Age and microchip revolution.

to residents cheaply, although in some Dene communities a few families are building their own, subsidized, log houses. The settlements are administered from Yellowknife following standard patterns: small ones are run by a (white) settlement manager, larger ones by an elected (mostly Native) council. Councils are charged now mostly with minor responsibilities, but political power is slowly devolving to give councils a say in such vital matters as education and local wildlife management.

Small industries such as log milling and com-

Nahanni Butte is a small Indian village near the confluence of the Nahanni and Liard rivers.
(Richard Harrington)

Signs of a successful hunting season lean against the wall of this house at Pangnirtung, an Inuit community of about 1,000 on Cumberland Sound, on the east coast of Baffin Island. Tourism, whale and seal hunting, and crafts such as carvings of bone and soapstone, support the area's residents.
(Lyn Hancock)

*The tiny community of Umingmaktok, or Bay Chimo, lies on the east side of Bathurst Inlet on the arctic coast. The Hudson's Bay Co. moved its trading post here in 1964; in 1968 the post was closed, but residents remain in the area and continue to live by subsistence. (Richard Harrington)*

The main challenge for northern Natives is to create a synthesis of old ways and new. How this might be done is one of the main preoccupations of every settlement. Nobody has hit on a universal answer, but individuals are coming to tentative conclusions for their own families.

Isaac Aleekuk is one such individual. Aleekuk, 31, is a slim, wiry man with a slim, wiry moustache. He is also president of the Hunters and Trappers Association of Holman Island, an Inuit settlement of 346 people in the western Arctic. Until recently he and most other Holman Island men considered themselves seal hunters.

"We used to be able to make a living before the seal market got screwed up," he says. The European sealskin market collapsed last year following protests by animal-welfare groups against the seal pup harvest off Newfoundland.

"We still hunt a few seals to feed our dogs but there is hardly anything to do now," Aleekuk says. He takes out American polar bear hunters in spring, does a little fishing in summer, and ponders the future.

"People here used to plan just for the next season or just one day at a time, but we're starting to think ahead more. I don't plan any changes for myself. I don't have any education. But my daughter is doing good in school and I'm encouraging her to go on. My son I am teaching him what I know, but I might not encourage him to be a hunter the way things are going now."

Wilfred and Lucie Jackson do not see formal schooling as the answer for their children. A few years ago, Wilfred went back to fur trapping almost full time, instead of taking wage jobs connected with oil exploration around Fort Good Hope — a Dene settlement of 454 people on the Mackenzie River near the Arctic Circle. Wilfred, Lucie, and their 11 children have a house in Fort Good Hope but spend most of the year in the woods, trapping marten in fall and winter, trapping beaver in spring, and fishing in summer. It is the type of life Wilfred, now 45, lived as a boy — attending school only at breakup, freezeup and during the coldest weeks of winter.

"I can't remember very well how to write and I sort of regret that," he says, resting in a canvas tent near the Mackenzie foothills after a day on the trap line with his son Michael. "But bush life teaches you how to work. That's important. My oldest son, Dennis, is a good worker. He's trapping on his own this winter up at Little Chicago [to the north]. Lawrence is working at Norman Wells [for Esso Resources Canada, 100 miles south of Fort Good Hope] making $15 an hour. A lot of boys don't last there, but Lawrence knows how to work and he stays with it. If he ever loses his job, he can go back to bush life."

Lucie, who reads and writes English well, says she would like her children to get a good education. But the elementary school in Fort Good Hope is mediocre compared to the mission school she attended as a child, she says. And the high school in Inuvik damaged her four eldest boys. "When they came back from that place after one year, they were not alive anymore, their mind and spirit were just dead. All the kids from Good Hope have the same experiences."

So the Jackson strategy is this: teach the children bush life; if trapping fails, they know hard work and can get a job; if they get laid off, they can survive in the Bush.

*An elderly Dene woman strings beads at Jean Marie River, population 49, south of Fort Simpson on the Mackenzie River in southern Northwest Territories. Women of the village are known for the quality of their traditional Dene crafts. (Lyn Hancock)*

Father Adam, shown here in 1972, pushes a wheelbarrow of soil outside the Igloo Church at Inuvik, with which he was associated until his death several years ago. Inuvik, population about 3,000, is the largest Canadian community north of the Arctic Circle. The community is connected to the rest of North America by the Dempster Highway which leads about 460 miles (743 kilometers) southwest to a point near Dawson City, Yukon Territory. *(Lyn Hancock)*

Driftwood is just one of the hazards of playing golf at the annual tournament at Tuktoyaktuk on the Arctic Coast. *(Lyn Hancock)*

Workers construct duplexes at the Inuit village of Pangnirtung, population 907, on the south shore of the Cumberland Peninsula on the east coast of Baffin Island. *(Richard Harrington)*

124

*Neat rows of houses line the main street of
Sanikiluaq, population 349, only community on
the Belcher Islands in Hudson Bay.*
*(Richard Harrington)*

**Left** — *Koaha, from near Bay Chimo, displays his skill at drum dancing. Koaha makes kayaks and lives off the land at his home on Bathurst Inlet.* (Lyn Hancock)

*A young Inuk plays with a Christmas present in his modern home at Igloolik, population 777, on an island near the northern tip of Melville Peninsula.* (Robert Semeniuk)

*Traditional beadwork adorns these dancers from Fort McPherson.*
*(Lyn Hancock)*

The future of young people is also a concern of the Northwest Territories government. Until five years ago, the legislative assembly was a colonial-type body controlled by white people appointed by the federal government. Now, although the head of government is still a federal appointee, the assembly consists of 24 elected members representing all regions and ethnic groups. The executive leader of the council is Richard Nerysoo, a 30-year-old Dene born in the Bush near Fort McPherson. Educational reform is a top priority, and a special program is under way to promote the use of native languages. The assembly also supports the three native land-claims organizations — representing the western Inuit, eastern Inuit, and Dene-Metis — in their negotiations with the federal government, to ensure long-term cultural security and economic prosperity for northern Natives.

Economic development is another priority. A long-anticipated oil boom in the Beaufort Sea and Arctic Islands still appears years away, so the government intends to help establish small companies and businesses in the settlements. The aim is to create jobs and training opportunities, especially for young people — for the Walkers.

*A youngster from Cape Dorset, near the entrance to Hudson Bay, can look forward to a challenging future as old and new come together on the ever-changing frontier of Canada's Northwest Territories. (Fred Bruemmer)*

# Alaska Geographic® Back Issues

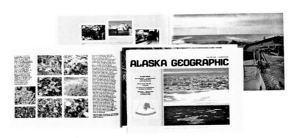

**The North Slope, Vol. 1, No. 1.** The charter issue of *ALASKA GEOGRAPHIC*® took a long, hard look at the North Slope and the then-new petroleum development at ''the top of the world.'' *Out of print.*

**One Man's Wilderness, Vol. 1, No. 2.** The story of a dream shared by many, fulfilled by a few; a man goes into the Bush, builds a cabin and shares his incredible wilderness experience. Color photos. 116 pages, $9.95.

**Admiralty . . . Island in Contention, Vol. 1, No. 3.** An intimate and multifaceted view of Admiralty: its geological and historical past, its present-day geography, wildlife and sparse human population. Color photos. 78 pages, $5.00

**Fisheries of the North Pacific: History, Species, Gear & Processes, Vol. 1, No. 4.** The title says it all. This volume is out of print, but the book, from which it was excerpted, is available in a revised, expanded large-format volume. 424 pages. $24.95.

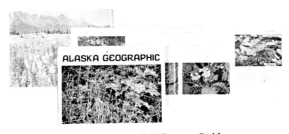

**The Alaska-Yukon Wild Flowers Guide, Vol. 2, No. 1.** First Northland flower book with both large, color photos and detailed drawings of every species described. Features 160 species, common and scientific names and growing height. Vertical-format book edition now available. 218 pages, $12.95.

**Richard Harrington's Yukon, Vol. 2, No. 2.** The Canadian province with the colorful past *and* present. *Out of print.*

**Prince William Sound, Vol. 2, No. 3.** This volume explores the people and resources of the Sound. *Out of print.*

**Yakutat: The Turbulent Crescent, Vol. 2, No. 4.** History, geography, people — and the impact of the coming of the oil industry. *Out of print.*

**Glacier Bay: Old Ice, New Land, Vol. 3, No. 1.** The expansive wilderness of southeastern Alaska's Glacier Bay National Monument (recently proclaimed a national park and preserve) unfolds in crisp text and color photographs. Records the flora and fauna of the area, its natural history, with hike and cruise information, plus a large-scale color map. 132 pages, $11.95.

**The Land: Eye of the Storm, Vol. 3, No. 2.** The future of one of the earth's biggest pieces of real estate! *This volume is out of print,* but the latest on the Alaska lands controversy is detailed completely in Volume 8, Number 4.

**Richard Harrington's Antarctic, Vol. 3, No. 3.** The Canadian photojournalist guides readers through remote and little understood regions of the Antarctic and Subantarctic. More than 200 color photos and a large fold-out map. 104 pages, $8.95

**The Silver Years of the Alaska Canned Salmon Industry: An Album of Historical Photos, Vol. 3, No. 4.** The grand and glorious past of the Alaska canned salmon industry. *Out of print.*

**Alaska's Volcanoes: Northern Link in the Ring of Fire, Vol. 4, No. 1.** Scientific overview supplemented with eyewitness accounts of Alaska's historic volcano eruptions. Includes color and black-and-white photos and a schematic description of the effects of plate movement upon volcanic activity. 88 pages. *Temporarily out of print.*

**The Brooks Range: Environmental Watershed, Vol. 4, No. 2.** An impressive work on a truly impressive piece of Alaska — The Brooks Range. *Out of print.*

**Kodiak: Island of Change, Vol. 4, No. 3.** Russians, wildlife, logging and even petroleum . . . an island where change is one of the few constants. *Out of print.*

**Wilderness Proposals: Which Way for Alaska's Lands? Vol. 4, No. 4.** This volume gives yet another detailed analysis of the many Alaska lands questions. *Out of print.*

**Cook Inlet Country, Vol. 5, No. 1.** Our first comprehensive look at the area. A visual tour of the region — its communities, big and small, and its countryside. Begins at the southern tip of the Kenai Peninsula, circles Turnagain Arm and Knik Arm for a close-up view of Anchorage, and visits the Matanuska and Susitna valleys and the wild, west side of the inlet. *Out of print.*

**Southeast: Alaska's Panhandle, Vol. 5, No. 2.** Explores southeastern Alaska's maze of fjords and islands, mossy forests and glacier-draped mountains — from Dixon Entrance to Icy Bay, including all of the state's fabled Inside Passage. Along the way are profiles of every town, together with a look at the region's history, economy, people, attractions and future. Includes large fold-out map and seven area maps. 192 pages, $12.95.

**Bristol Bay Basin, Vol. 5, No. 3.** Explores the land and the people of the region known to many as the commercial salmon-fishing capital of Alaska. Illustrated with contemporary color and historic black-and-white photos. Includes a large fold-out map of the region. *Out of print.*

**Alaska Whales and Whaling, Vol. 5, No. 4.** The wonders of whales in Alaska — their life cycles, travels and travails — are examined, with an authoritative history of commercial and subsistence whaling in the North. Includes a fold-out poster of 14 major whale species in Alaska in perspective, color photos and illustrations, with historical photos and line drawings. 144 pages, $12.95.

**Yukon-Kuskokwim Delta, Vol. 6, No. 1.** This volume explores the people and life-styles of one of the most remote areas of the 49th state. *Out of print.*

**The Aurora Borealis, Vol. 6, No. 2.** Here one of the world's leading experts — Dr. S.-I. Akasofu of the University of Alaska — explains in an easily understood manner, aided by many diagrams and spectacular color and black-and-white photos, what causes the aurora, how it works, how and why scientists are studying it today and its implications for our future. 96 pages, $7.95.

**Alaska's Native People, Vol. 6, No. 3.** In this edition the editors examine the varied worlds of the Inupiat Eskimo, Yup'ik Eskimo, Athabascan, Aleut, Tlingit, Haida and Tsimshian. Included are sensitive, informative articles by Native writers, plus a large, four-color map detailing the Native villages and defining the language areas. 304 pages, $24.95.

**The Stikine, Vol. 6, No. 4.** River route to three Canadian gold strikes in the 1800s. This edition explores 400 miles of Stikine wilderness, recounts the river's paddle-wheel past and looks into the future. Illustrated with contemporary color photos and historic black-and-white; includes a large fold-out map. 96 pages, $9.95.

**Alaska's Great Interior, Vol. 7, No. 1.** Alaska's rich Interior country, west from the Alaska-Yukon Territory border and including the huge drainage between the Alaska Range and the Brooks Range, is covered thoroughly. Included are the region's people, communities, history, economy, wilderness areas and wildlife. Illustrated with contemporary color and black-and-white photos. Includes a large fold-out map. 128 pages, $9.95.

**A Photographic Geography of Alaska,** Vol. 7, No. 2. An overview of the entire state — a visual tour through the six regions of Alaska: Southeast, Southcentral/Gulf Coast, Alaska Peninsula and Aleutians, Bering Sea Coast, Arctic and Interior. Plus a handy appendix of valuable information — ''Facts About Alaska.'' Approximately 160 color and black-and-white photos and 35 maps. 192 pages. Revised in 1983. $15.95.

**The Aleutians, Vol. 7, No. 3.** Home of the Aleut, a tremendous wildlife spectacle, a major World War II battleground and now the heart of a thriving new commercial fishing industry. Contemporary color and black-and-white photographs, and a large fold-out map. 224 pages, $14.95.

**Klondike Lost: A Decade of Photographs by Kinsey & Kinsey, Vol. 7, No. 4.** An album of rare photographs and all-new text about the lost Klondike boomtown of Grand Forks, second in size only to Dawson during the gold rush. Introduction by noted historian Pierre Berton: 138 pages, area maps and more than 100 historical photos, most never before published. $12.95.

**Wrangell-Saint Elias, Vol. 8, No. 1.** Mountains, including the continent's second- and fourth-highest peaks, dominate this international wilderness that sweeps from the Wrangell Mountains in Alaska to the southern Saint Elias range in Canada. Illustrated with contemporary color and historical black-and-white photographs. Includes a large fold-out map. 144 pages, $9.95.

**Alaska Mammals, Vol. 8, No. 2.** From tiny ground squirrels to the powerful polar bear, and from the tundra hare to the magnificent whales inhabiting Alaska's waters, this volume includes 80 species of mammals found in Alaska. Included are beautiful color photographs and personal accounts of wildlife encounters. 184 pages, $12.95.

**The Kotzebue Basin, Vol. 8, No. 3.** Examines northwestern Alaska's thriving trading area of Kotzebue Sound and the Kobuk and Noatak river basins. Contemporary color and historical black-and-white photographs. 184 pages, $12.95.

**Alaska National Interest Lands, Vol. 8, No. 4.** Following passage of the bill formalizing Alaska's national interest land selections (d-2 lands), longtime Alaskans Celia Hunter and Ginny Wood review each selection, outlining location, size, access, and briefly describing the region's special attractions. Illustrated with contemporary color photographs. 242 pages, $14.95.

**Alaska's Glaciers, Vol. 9, No. 1.** Examines in-depth the massive rivers of ice, their composition, exploration, present-day distribution and scientific significance. Illustrated with many contemporary color and historical black-and-white photos, the text includes separate discussions of more than a dozen glacial regions. 144 pages, $9.95.

**Sitka and Its Ocean/Island World, Vol. 9, No. 2.** From the elegant capital of Russian America to a beautiful but modern port, Sitka, on Baranof Island, has become a commercial and cultural center for southeastern Alaska. Pat Roppel, longtime Southeast resident and expert on the region's history, examines in detail the past and present of Sitka, Baranof Island, and neighboring Chichagof Island. Illustrated with contemporary color and historical black-and-white photographs. 128 pages, $9.95.

**Islands of the Seals: The Pribilofs, Vol. 9, No. 3.** Great herds of northern fur seals drew Russians and Aleuts to these remote Bering Sea islands where they founded permanent communities and established a unique international commerce. Illustrated with contemporary color and historical black-and-white photographs. 128 pages. $9.95.

**Alaska's Oil/Gas & Minerals Industry, Vol. 9, No. 4.** Experts detail the geological processes and resulting mineral and fossil fuel resources that are now in the forefront of Alaska's economy. Illustrated with historical black-and-white and contemporary color photographs. 216 pages. $12.95.

**Adventure Roads North: The Story of the Alaska Highway and Other Roads in *The MILEPOST* ®, Vol. 10, No. 1.** From Alaska's first highway — the Richardson — to the famous Alaska Highway, first overland route to the 49th state, text and photos provide a history of Alaska's roads and take a mile-by-mile look at the country they cross. 224 pages. $14.95.

**ANCHORAGE and the Cook Inlet Basin . . . Alaska's Commercial Heartland, Vol. 10, No. 2.** An update of what's going on in "Anchorage country" . . . the Kenai, the Susitna Valley, and Matanuska. Heavily illustrated in color and including three illustrated maps . . . one an uproarious artist's forecast of "Anchorage 2035." 168 pages. $14.95.

**Alaska's Salmon Fisheries, Vol. 10, No. 3.** The work of *ALASKA*® magazine outdoors editor Jim Rearden, this issue takes a comprehensive look at Alaska's most valuable commercial fishery. Through text and photos, readers will learn about the five species of salmon caught in Alaska, different types of fishing gear and how each works, and will take a district-by-district tour of salmon fisheries throughout the state. 128 pages. $12.95.

**Koyukuk Country, Vol. 10, No. 4.** This issue explores the vast drainage of the Koyukuk River, third largest in Alaska. Text and photos provide information on the land and offer insights into the life-style of the people who live and have lived along the Koyukuk. 152 pages. $14.95.

**Nome: City of the Golden Beaches, Vol. 11, No. 1.** The colorful history of Alaska's most famous gold rush town has never been told like this before. With a text written by Terrence Cole, and illustrated with hundreds of rare black-and-white photos, the book traces the story of Nome from the crazy days of the 1900 gold rush. 184 pages. $14.95.

**Alaska's Farms and Gardens, Vol. 11, No. 2.** An overview of the past, present, and future of agriculture in Alaska, and a wealth of information on how to grow your own fruit and vegetables in the north. 144 pages. $12.95.

**Chilkat River Valley, Vol. 11, No. 3.** Its strategic location at the head of the Inside Passage has long made the Chilkat Valley a corridor between the coast and Interior. This issue explores the mountain-rimmed valley, its natural resources, and those hardy residents who make their home along the Chilkat. 112 pages. $12.95.

**ALASKA STEAM, A Pictorial History of the Alaska Steamship Company, Vol. 11, No. 4.** An inspiring story by Northwest history writer, Lucile McDonald, of men and ships who pioneered the hazardous waters of the northern travel lanes to serve the people of Alaska. Over 100 black-and-white historical photographs. 160 pages, $12.95.

**All prices U.S. funds.**

**NEXT ISSUE:**

**Alaska's Forest Resources, Vol. 12, No. 2.** This issue examines Alaska's majestic and valuable forests, which cover about one-third of the state's land area. Contributing editor Walt Matell presents an in-depth look at the subject, with informative, easy-to-read text and nearly 200 historical black-and-white and contemporary color photos. Topics include silviculture, the science of growing trees; a history of the timber industry in Alaska; how to identify the state's 33 native tree species; forest fires; traditional uses of Alaska's forests; and modern timber-harvesting techniques. To members in May 1985. Price to be announced.

## The Alaska Geographic Society

Box 4-EEE, Anchorage, AK 99509

Membership in The Alaska Geographic Society is $30 (U.S. funds), and includes the following year's four quarterlies which explore a wide variety of subjects in the Northland, each issue an adventure in great photos, maps, and excellent research. Members receive their quarterlies as part of the membership fee at considerable savings over the prices which nonmembers must pay for individual book editions.